INSIDE BBC SCOTLAND
1975–1980

A PERSONAL VIEW

Alastair Hetherington

WHITEWATER PRESS

First published 1992
Whitewater Press
© Alastair Hetherington 1992

BRITISH LIBRARY CATALOGUING-IN-PUBLICATION DATA

A catalogue record for this book is available from the British Library

ISBN: 0-9519619-0-X

Typeset from author-generated discs by BPCC-AUP Glasgow Ltd
Printed by BPCC-AUP Aberdeen Ltd

Foreword

Here is a brief broadcasting autobiography by a distinguished Scot which should find its specific niche in what is by now an extensive tradition of such writing.

I first read it two days before the General Election of 9 April 1992. The prevailing political atmosphere in Scotland at that moment led many to believe that significant constitutional change was on the cards. Undoubtedly, that mood coloured my reading, and made me think that Alastair Hetherington's candid tale about the relations between BBC Scotland and its London HQ during the 1970s might indeed be retold by someone else in the 1990s.

Now I am not quite so sure. What I do remain certain of, however, is that the story is worth telling, and required reading for all who are interested in the politics of broadcasting and, more generally, in the contemporary politics of culture in Scotland.

At a different level, unreconstructed centralisers in government who influence cultural policy and practice would do well to take the message on board—and not only in England. This is a time when European economic and political integration is being paralleled by a contrary tendency of ethno-national mobilisation throughout the continent. Those who think broadcasting has an important role to play in the construction of cultural and national identity will certainly find this an instructive case study.

It is above all a tale of political, economic and cultural dependency, instantly recognisable to those who inhabit nations without states— and also to those who live in small independent states which import their audiovisual culture.

It only remains to say that the dilemmas posed here by the author may simply not disappear. If the present government does decide to opt for some form of devolution, relations between Scottish broadcasting generally and politics in Scotland will—and must—change. If such change is on the way, here at least is one account to turn to from which something can be learned about policy and organisational questions. If the status quo prevails—well that's another story.

Philip Schlesinger
Stirling, 3 May 1992
(Professor Philip Schlesinger
Department of Film and Media Studies
Stirling University)

Contents

Foreword   Professor Philip Schlesinger

Chapter 1   The political atmosphere, 1975, and views of the future   1

Chapter 2   Transmitters, Frequencies and 'Opt outs'   15

Chapter 3   Drama, Northern Isles, and our network programmes   20

Chapter 4   The Broadcasting Council for Scotland, the DG explodes, but better days come   28

Chapter 5   Lilybank   43

Chapter 6   The Nation and its Future   47

Chapter 7   Church and Nation   56

Chapter 8   Gaelic, Farming, Music, Money and Sport   62

Chapter 9   A real Radio Scotland, at last   71

Chapter 10   The bad and the good   77

    Appendix 1   91

    Appendix 2   92

Acknowledgements

Many people helped to revive my memory, and in other ways. I especially wish to thank David Barlow, Kenneth Cargill, Patrick Chalmers, Martin Dalby, Aileen Forsyth, Neil Fraser, Mary Heaney, Malcolm Kellard, Ian Mackenzie, David Martin, Bryan Mitchell, Philip Schlesinger, Matt Spicer, Kay Weaver.

They are not to blame for any errors.

Some prominent characters

Noel Annan (Lord Annan), Provost of University College, London and later Vice Chancellor; *chairman, Committee on the Future of Broadcasting, 1974–77*.

Lady Avonside (Janet Shearer), *Scottish Governor, BBC, 1971–76*. Wife of Lord Avonside, a Senator of the College of Justice in Scotland

Sir Charles Curran, *Director General of the BBC 1969–77*. Previously Director of External Broadcasting

Alasdair Milne, *Managing Director BBC Tv, 1977–82*, and BBC Director General 1982–86. Previously Controller BBC Scotland, 1968–72; Director of Programmes (Tv) 1973–77.

Rt Hon William Ross MP, *Secretary of State for Scotland 1964–70 and 1974–76*; later Lord Ross of Marnock.

Sir Michael Swann, *Chairman of BBC Governors, 1973–80*. Previously Principal and Vice-Chancellor, University of Edinburgh 1965–73; later Lord Swann.

Sir Ian Trethowan, *Director General 1977–82*. Managing Director Radio, 1969–75; MD Tv 1976–77. Earlier, political correspondent *Yorkshire Post*; *News Chronicle*; Political Editor, ITV; BBC as commentator, politics and current affairs 1963–9

Chapter 1

The political atmosphere, 1975, and views of the future

> *The point about public service broadcasting is that it makes culture and communication universally available. The broadcasting signal reaches everyone, universally, at the same price wherever they live. The programmes that are offered cover the widest possible range ...*
>
> Janet Morgan, *at the Hamburg Intermedia Conference, 1985.*

'You're mad', said David English, editor of the *Daily Mail*, when he heard that I was to leave *The Guardian* and go to BBC Scotland. He did not approve of public service broadcasting and he disliked the BBC. 'It will destroy you', he said. I disagreed. I had been the editor of *The Guardian* for 19 years, first in charge of the old *Manchester Guardian* from the autumn of 1956 and then taking the retitled *Guardian* to London in 1961. I loved the work, but I wanted a change, and above all I wanted to return to Scotland. I had (and still have) great respect for the BBC, and the opportunity came through Sir Michael Swann, then Chairman of the Governors of the BBC.

In Scotland 1975 was a fascinating time. A new dynamism had come to Scottish politics. Today it is hard to recall the political atmosphere of that time—or was until the sudden revival of Scottish expectations in the winter of 1991 and spring of 1992. The two general elections of 1974 had seen a dramatic increase in the strength of the Scottish National Party—with seven seats in Parliament after the February conflict and 11 in October. At that October election, in Scotland, Labour won 41 seats and the Conservatives 16. The Labour Party itself, after years of opposition to any form of Scottish self-government, had switched to supporting 'elected assemblies' for Scotland and Wales. Even the Conservatives were moving in that direction; and the Liberals had long wanted an Assembly or Scottish Parliament. Some form of self-government seemed certain.

That winter Sir Michael Swann asked me whether I would run the

BBC's Scottish operation. He knew that I wanted to return to Scotland, to an academic or other fresh post. With a Scottish Assembly in the offing, he believed that broadcasting in Scotland might well be removed from the BBC's control. He wanted to avoid that, if possible, and he wanted someone with strong political experience for the post of Controller Scotland (the top BBC post in Scotland). The post was vacant. Seven applicants had been interviewed and all had been turned down. Now Swann had decided to take matters into his own hands, although Charles Curran as Director General was less than happy at someone with no BBC background coming in.

Because Swann wanted someone with political experience, he approached me. I could not answer at once because of *Guardian* and related commitments. At the time I was leading the national newspapers collectively in securing a revision of the Government's proposed trade union law, and then I had to lead the *Guardian*'s case with the Inland Revenue on the newspaper's unique position as a non-profitmaking Trust. These were completed by late February, and in early March of 1975 I accepted Swann's offer. The appointment was to take effect in the autumn. After two months of 'initiation', mainly in London, on Tuesday 2nd December 1975 I took up my office in the BBC Scotland headquarters in Glasgow.

The political atmosphere may well be seen from a private talk with the Secretary of State for Scotland, William Ross, in his room at the House of Commons in October 1975. He was in a cheerful mood, in spite of Labour's narrow majority (Lab 319; all others together 316). On the subject of the proposed Scottish Assembly, he was both caustic and serious: it would be full of 'nabobs' and Edinburgh lawyers, though he admitted that it would be easier to get good candidates for the Assembly than for Westminster. As to whether there would be an Assembly, he appeared to have no doubts, but he had no immediate comment on whether broadcasting in Scotland would come within the Assembly's duties. We went on to a lengthy discussion on other broadcasting matters, in particular his belief that there should be more small local radio stations in Scotland, with which I fully agreed. Of that and other problems, more will come later.

That meeting was in late October of 1975, soon after I had joined the BBC. We had a further talk in Edinburgh shortly before Christmas. By then I had a clearer view of what a Scottish Assembly might mean to broadcasters (to the BBC, ITV and independent radio, that is). The Government had published its White Paper, but that did not state whether broadcasting would go to the Assembly. Ross said that it probably would. The Annan Committee at that time was well advanced in its UK report on *The Future of Broadcasting*.

Urged on by Sir Michael Swann, in February 1976 I had a private talk with Lord Annan, whom I had known for many years. Towards the end of that meeting, he said it would be very helpful to his committee if I would put on paper some of my comments on management between the BBC in London and in Scotland. One of his Scottish members had been pressing for something of the kind, to supplement the BBC's earlier submissions. He was Sir James Mackay, now retired after many years in the Admiralty and then in the Home Office in London, and more recently the deputy chairman of the Highlands and Islands Development Board. He lived near Inverness and had strong views about the future of the BBC in Scotland.

Having been only five months within the Corporation, I would have preferred to wait, but Annan's report was far advanced. So I drafted a summary—no more than one and a half pages, but with a three page 'annexure' to provide more detail. It was headed 'BBC Scotland's *mini-devolution*, a phrase borrowed from the Director-General, Sir Charles Curran, who had used it before I joined the BBC, and on 16 February I sent copies of the draft to Sir Michael Swann and to Sir Charles. Swann approved of my draft immediately, asking for no changes. The 'DG', Curran, took a different view.

Whereas Swann and Annan both understood the political pressures in Scotland, Curran was reluctant to take much account of them. Although he had been the first to use the term *mini-devolution*, he was not prepared to give much ground. He received my draft on Thursday 19 February (the same day as Swann) and next day sent a message saying that he had given copies to all his Board of Management for comment at his next Monday meeting.

That Monday I was due to meet, for the first time, the Church of Scotland's Church and Nation Committee. They had asked for the meeting because they believed that BBC Scotland was not giving them the time or quality of cover that they deserved, though they themselves were not in agreement about whether they wanted more live broadcasts of church services or (as on the whole preferred by the BBC in Scotland) specially organised programmes with ministers, laymen and broadcasters together. It was a matter that must be taken seriously. I had been well briefed by our Head of Religion, and I wanted to listen carefully at the meeting, which was held in their George Street office in Edinburgh.

That meeting began about 2.20, when the committee had finished other business. At about 2.40, when the discussion had barely begun, a worried Church secretary came in with a message for me. It was from the DG (Curran), saying that I must return at once to Glasgow, to take part in a round-table discussion with all his management group. Arrangements were being made for a 'secured' radio link from the basement at Broadcasting House in London to a safely remote room in BBC Scotland in Glasgow. The twelve in the London radio room were to speak to me, and hear me, while I was by myself in Glasgow. The discussion was to start at 4pm and I must be there.

Greatly embarrassed, I had to tell my hosts that I would have to leave in about ten minutes. The discussion had to be postponed. It was, to my mind, wounding to them and to me. We did eventually meet again some weeks later, but it illustrated rather pointedly the remoteness of London from matters which were important to Scotland and its people.

Back in Glasgow an hour later, I found that the engineers, on instructions from London, had set up the special radio link in a small room high in the oldest part of the old Queen Margaret building. There I sat for more than ninety minutes while the objections to my draft were put forward. (One irony, disclosed to me long afterwards, was that in Birmingham, through which the link went, some staff had listened to bits of it in amazement: so much for the 'security'.) In the end I agreed to rephrase a number of points, but I refused to remove any of them totally. They had been passed by the chairman of the BBC's Governors. They were in line with what I had discussed with the DG in early January. I believed them to be sound.

It was a painful afternoon, and relations were never really restored. The DG had never been as open with me as the chairman was, and of course it had been Swann who had approached me about the possibility of joining the BBC. One consolation was that, in addition to sending my draft to the chairman and the DG, I had sent a copy to the chairman of the Broadcasting Council for Scotland—the body of twelve outside people who were supposed to monitor BBC Scotland's work. At the next meeting of the BCS, three days after that painful afternoon, Lady Avonside told those present that my paper was 'splendid' and that it would be available for discussion at the next meeting. She said that she 'strongly supported' what I had said and that she had written to Sir Michael saying so.

What were the points that Curran disliked? In the end it took over two weeks of exchanges with the BBC's Assistant Secretary in London, speaking for the DG, before we agreed a revised version of my note for the Annan Committee. By then the document had doubled in length.

Two views of the future

You may wonder why I give such priority to the Annan affair and to Sir Charles Curran's hostile reaction. To me, I had done no more than try to look ahead at likely events in Scotland—with the Assembly and all that must go with it—and at the best way for the BBC to act in its own interests. As already noted, Sir Michael Swann took no exception to my paper. He understood the realities in Scotland—the pressure towards a measure of Scottish devolution. The Director General, while having said that BBC Scotland must have 'mini-devolution', was in no way willing to provide for it. At one point he had declared 'I take the decisions; you follow my orders'.

To underline the difference between us, I summarise below the main points of my paper. Readers may make their own judgments. The summary at least indicates what I believed that the BBC must face. It was, of course, originally drafted for Lord Annan and Sir James Mackay, and it had been approved by Sir Michael Swann.

In essence it said that we must be prepared for a Scottish Assembly, that BBC Scotland must have more freedom to decide for itself the way its money was used, and that its first priority must be that of strengthening news and current affairs. The main points were these:

'Mini-devolution'. A year before, about the time when I had agreed to leave *The Guardian* and return to Scotland, the BBC in London had stated publicly that it intended 'to pursue a policy of giving greater autonomy to Scotland.' Six months later the Government published its White Paper *'Our Changing Democracy'*, which was much criticised in Scotland for not going far enough and in England for going too far. It was evident, however, that the new Scottish Assembly was likely to demand control over broadcasting in Scotland. We must be prepared for this. My own view was that 'there is real value for Scotland in retaining a close link with the rest of the BBC'. In my three months in Scotland the BBC's movements had been 'perhaps more cautious than you or I would wish' ('you' being Sir James Mackay).

'Transmitters'. At that time UHF television was available only in Central Scotland and parts of the north-east, and even in these areas there were serious gaps. The rest of Scotland depended on the old 405-line transmitters—hence the demand for the new 625-line systems. These were matters wholly controlled from London, and Scotland had been 'generously treated'. Nevertheless, in the long term these decisions on priorities might have to be taken in Scotland. (UHF was only just about to reach Sir James's Loch Ness.)

'Capital projects'. These, too, were wholly controlled from London. They involved new buildings, new centres such as at Inverness, and any major equipment newly developed. We readily accepted all that.

'Operating expenditure'. The BBC's stated view was that BBC Scotland

enjoyed 'a substantial budget of its own', while London was involved only with 'new money'. In theory that was good practice, but 'it is hard, if not impossible, to find anyone in the BBC in Scotland who will entirely endorse that view'. (In other words BBC Scotland was not free to take financial decisions without detailed approval from London.)

'Administration'. BBC staff in Scotland tended to believe that parts of the London administration—not all—were 'slow and paternalistic'. The London reply tended to suggest that administration in Scotland was 'not always competent'. My view was that there must be greater administrative devolution, not least on appointments. 'There are', I said, 'one or two little time bombs ticking away, but it remains to be seen who (if anyone) will be blown up'.

My original 'Administration' section had been short and mild, but the DG was much irritated by it. It remained short but sharper, with 'streamlining' of the Admin system as a priority. In the end, of course, it was I who was blown up.

'Programme making'. My draft had said that access to network time was 'vital' if we were to be seen as part of the UK. This was extended and toned down in the DG's version, so that it put first Scotland's 'freedom to devise its own output for Scottish use' and then said that for the 'big money' network programmes a greater access could be expected within the next 12 to 18 months. (That promise was honoured in part the following year.)

'News and Current Affairs'. This section remained intact, with my hope for a strengthened Scottish staff and the addition of specialist correspondents.

To my mind, the key words in this document were 'streamlining' and 'mini-devolution'—the first because it provoked the most angry reply from the Director of Personnel, although that had been mentioned only in one sentence at the end of my first draft for the Annan Committee, and 'mini-devolution' because it was at the heart of the planning for the BBC in Scotland if or when a political Scottish Assembly came. The 'streamlining' was an internal BBC matter, much needed in my view. The 'devolution' was unavoidable if the BBC was to face the intentions of the Labour Government, the Liberals, and the growing Scottish National Party. The Secretary of State for Scotland had seen me again in London in early February; Jo Grimond, as leader of the Liberals, together with Russell Johnston had spoken to me in favour of the Assembly; and the SNP, at their own request, had had a long talk with me. The SNP had gone so far as to say that if they won 36 or more seats at the next election they would go beyond the

Assembly to a 'confederal' transition, which would inevitably mean a Scottish Broadcasting Authority appointed by the Scottish Government.

Though I had no wish whatever to see BBC Scotland separated from the rest of the BBC, I had to tell the SNP that if they went for separation they would have to buy a lot of programmes from the BBC, much as the Irish broadcasters did in Dublin. They were not bothered by that, saying that they would have a three-channel system with one commercial service (buying out the shareholders of STV and Grampian if necessary) and two 'public' services—though this was not yet agreed party policy. They admitted that the licence fee would have to be higher than the BBC's licence, since they would have to provide for the transmitters as well as programmes.

Lest there be any misunderstanding, the absence of Conservatives does not imply disregard. I had had, and continued to have, meetings with Scottish Conservatives—Gordon Campbell (Secretary of State for Scotland 1970–74), George Younger, Alex Fletcher and Michael Ancram among them—but the talk was about broader Scottish affairs. The Conservatives complained about others receiving more air time, as almost all MPs did (including William Ross, who got more time than anyone else), but the Conservatives had no immediate plans for changes in the BBC. That at least was a relief.

The specialists come

My problem at that time was with the Director General and some of his colleagues. The directors of television and radio and their deputies were in general helpful and friendly, though the BBC system left Scotland, Wales and Northern Ireland at a disadvantage. Until then the three Controllers had accepted the metropolitan domination. I believed that there must be change, in the BBC's own interests. My most immediate problems apart from the DG were the directors of personnel and finance. (Staffing and administration came under personnel.) I had separate lunches with each soon after the DG conflict, one in London and the other in Glasgow. Each afterwards wrote me charming letters: but neither was ready to move an inch from his position. That was the BBC. (In Glasgow, after lunch and talk with the director of personnel, I took him for a car ride to the Trossachs, Stirling Castle and Bannockburn, which, on a beautiful spring day, I enjoyed at least as much as he did. Bannockburn had been chosen for reasons that all Scots understand.)

'Streamlining the administration' had become my top priority for the moment, DG or no DG. Before I joined the BBC I had asked for only one thing—the appointment of four specialist correspondents to strengthen Scottish news and current affairs. Until then there had been no specialists, though there were some first class reporters—and some duds. Yet five months after I had joined the BBC and three months after moving to Glasgow we had managed to appoint only one of the four.

I had asked for correspondents for politics, economics, the environment and countryside, and UK energy, including offshore oil and industrial development. By the end of February only the energy correspondent had been chosen—Michael Buerk, now well known for his work in many parts of the world—and he was expected to be based in Glasgow by Easter. The political post had been advertised, but there had been no interviews as yet. The other two had not yet been advertised. The Glasgow administration said it was London's fault, while London said it was Glasgow's. It was probably a bit of both, and it was many months more before there was any real improvement.

The political post was filled later that year, after interviews with some very good candidates. It went to Chris Baur, then the Scottish correspondent of the *Financial Times*. Once established, he was much in demand by the London programmes—as intended—and was greatly overworked. Eventually he insisted, quite rightly, that he should take on only the bigger events and the longer programmes. One of the last programmes he made, a one-hour BBC 2 network called *Power of Scotland* (about the Scottish Office and the Secretary of State) won the UK Royal Television Society's Journalism Award for 'the best current affairs-documentary programme of 1978.' After that, to my great regret, he left to return to newspaper work. While with us he was still under extreme pressure from tv and radio in London, and he wanted to write and comment in greater depth than he found possible in the BBC.

The third appointment, later still, was economics. Of those who were interviewed, one candidate seemed to me to stand out. She was Helen Liddell, who for five years after graduating at Strathclyde University had been head of the economics department of the Scottish Trade Union Council. But there was a problem: having been brought up in Coatbridge, she had a warm mid-Scotland accent, which would apparently be unacceptable for network programmes. The two London people at the interviews—who had been sent north to monitor what we did in Scotland—were clear about that. So I decided to make no appointment then, but with approval from London I took her on with a six-month contract as a trainee and then, if needed, a further six months as a reporter. In addition, to satisfy London, since National Controllers were given £5000 a year to use as they wished (Huw

Wheldon had told me it could be used mainly for giving parties), I paid for Helen to be speech-trained out of working hours. She took to it magnificently, developing two completely different styles—one for English consumption, the other for Scotland.

In the late autumn, since she was doing so well, we tried to have her appointed to a permanent post. That was blocked from London, although the two from London who came for the interview board supported her. Then in the early spring we advertised the economics correspondent's post again. Once again there was no doubt about the best applicant. But this time the two from London—one from the top level at television news and one from administration—had come north with instructions to block her appointment. I had not known of that until after the interviews, and I tried by telephone to get the block lifted. To no avail. The final irony was that next day, before she knew the result, Helen Liddell did an excellent report from McDermott's big offshore construction yard in Ardersier, which led the UK news both at 6pm and at 9pm. Back in Glasgow, having heard the result, she resigned at once: a great loss to the BBC.

The reason for the blocking of Mrs Liddell from London was never made clear. At that time there were suggestions that Andrew Boyle was behind the objection, but that seems unlikely. Boyle was then acting in Glasgow as temporary Head of News and Current Affairs. When I had been about to move north in the winter of 1975, Charles Curran asked me to accept him for some months, until other arrangements for BBC Scotland could be made. Curran said Boyle would help to strengthen the Scottish team: he was of Scottish origin, though he had worked almost all of his life in London. (Later, in 1979, his book about the 'fourth man'—the spy Anthony Blunt—made Boyle well known.) He seemed helpful to the younger news and current affairs staff, though he generated little action himself. As long as he knew what was happening, he was content. And according to Helen Liddell herself Boyle was 'very supportive' to her.

The fourth post was never filled. Environment and countryside would have been valuable, but it was not to be. I did not want another fiasco.

Of the specialists, more comes in the later section 'News and Current Affairs'.

Lost time and money

Going back to the Annan Committee and Sir James Mackay, I kept in touch with Sir James, visiting him two or three times at his house overlooking Loch Ness. He was always invigorating, a strong supporter of the BBC's 'public service' principle, but highly critical of the delays in development in Scotland.

Lest Noel Annan or Sir James were to ask for more detail, in late February I had prepared, for my own use, a short list of difficulties caused by BBC procedures. (This was after the private talk with Lord Annan, noted earlier, and before the first big row with the Director General.) The first case, sparked by my wish for 'streamlining', was that when I had wanted to pay £800 of 'Scottish' money for a new style of type for tv titles and credits I'd had to notify 58 individual people in England before I could do it. The idea was that it might be possible to borrow the equipment from someone else, and that London, Birmingham and others must be consulted first. It was well meant, but a mad system, I thought, costing time and money and useless in relation to news and current affairs. In any event, was it a matter for the Controller? I thought that it was a matter for the Head of News in Glasgow, together with the administration there.

Other examples. 1) The four correspondents. Those had been agreed nine months earlier, in discussion before I joined the BBC, but so far only one had been appointed. 2) The Head of Drama, an upgraded post because of the expectation of more network programmes from Scotland. Because of its nature, the television centre in London had taken over the arrangements. Memos were going back and forward, to the embarrassment of myself and others in Scotland. 3) The Glasgow Queen Margaret Drive rubbish compactor, for collecting and destroying the trash. Three years earlier it had been agreed with London that a new one was needed. At that time it would have cost £1500. Now the cost would be £7500 or more, and administration in London said it was too expensive. The matter had been referred to me. 4) Grading the salaries of the two new posts for Orkney and Shetland. Nothing had happened, although in principle it had been blessed by Ian Trethowan before he moved from Director Radio to being Director Television. The Glasgow administration had slipped up in not pursuing the matter, but why should it have to go to London anyway? 5) One extra doorkey was wanted for the (then unmanned) Dundee studio. The indemnity had to be signed by the Director General in London, no less, after clearance by the London legal department. And, 6 to 12, I could offer as many examples again. It was all too trivial and incompetent. Heaven help us, I thought, when the Scottish Assembly comes.

When the Annan committee finally published its report in March of 1977, many interested people in Scotland (myself among them) were well pleased with it. It called for more programmes for the networks from BBC Scotland, Wales and Northern Ireland. It said that the three Controllers should have 'a greater say' over the scheduling in their areas, both for radio and television. It recommended that, although major projects such as the building of the proposed new Edinburgh centre must continue to be authorised centrally, Scotland and Wales should be given 'a limited annual budget for more minor capital investment'. (That has happened, but not on the scale that Annan implied.) Of these, more comes later in the 'Devolution' section.

Meanwhile, my dismay and irritation were sharpened by the contrast between the management of *The Guardian* and *Manchester Evening News* and the BBC. The rule at the *G & MEN* was that Board and other documents must be kept as short as possible, ideally not more than one or two pages, and that memoranda for lower levels should also be kept short. In principle, written papers were needed only when there might be call for reviewing decisions at a later date. That system worked well, meetings were kept short, and the minutes recorded decisions. The same applied to the Scott Trust, owners of all the ordinary shares of the company. Time was not wasted.

By contrast, the first time I was asked to write a paper for the BBC's Governors—on a secondary subject, but of interest in Scotland—I sent less than two pages (single spaced). On receiving it, the BBC's Chief Secretary telephoned to say that at least five pages were expected for the Governors. So I wrote five pages, which was not difficult. But what a waste of everyone's time.

Quite early in my time in BBC Scotland, I had said to the (London) directors of finance and personnel that if Scotland could appoint all of its own staff—except, say, the top six—and if we were to reorganise our staffing I could save the BBC at least £1m a year. From my *Guardian* experience I was sure of it. To them it was heresy. The centralised BBC could never contemplate it.

It may be said that *G & MEN* was a small operation compared with the BBC. True, in terms of staff directly under me; but as a director I had had to deal with budgets that were a great deal bigger than BBC Scotland's—and very much better handled. Later, when I had left the BBC, I became Chairman of the Scott Trust (owners of the *G & MEN*). It was a great pleasure to be involved in a much more effective operation. I cannot, of course, comment on any comparison today; but I well remember quiet groans from Michael Checkland, sitting close to me at BBC meetings. He was then Controller of Planning and Resource Management, and a very good one; now he is DG—and one of the best ever.

To the Front—News and Current Affairs

When I arrived in the winter of 1975 there were many talented men and women in the BBC in Glasgow, Edinburgh and Aberdeen. The two orchestras—the Scottish Symphony and the Scottish Radio Orchestra—were much enjoyed and were performing in many parts of Scotland. Drama was creative, both in television and in radio. Alasdair Milne, while Controller in Scotland between 1968 and 72, had concentrated on tv drama, bringing much of the output up to network standards for both BBC 1 and BBC 2. Light entertainment, though almost exclusively for Scottish audiences, was of a high standard—featuring, to name only a few, Anne Lorne Gillies, Peter Morrison, the McCalmans and Jimmie MacGregor. Religious broadcasts were extensive and often original, thanks to the exceptional skill and insight of Ian Mackenzie. Such criticism as there was came simultaneously from opposite directions of the religious divide. The radio 'features' people were also producing a wide range of good programmes. They needed nothing from me except thanks, encouragement and the continuing fight for more money.

My main concern, however, was with news and current affairs. Here again Michael Swann made it clear that there must be a rapid improvement in quality and quantity. Swann still had a house in Edinburgh—his main home, in fact—and he was there for two or three days in most weeks. His comments on the stodgy output were justified, as I soon discovered.

Patrick Walker, Head of Programmes, had for the past nine or ten months been Acting Controller. (The Controller before me had been ill throughout that time.) Pat Walker had had a hard time in those long months and he was relieved when I arrived. Pat was liked and much respected in BBC Scotland. He was not responsible for the 'stodgy output' from our newsrooms. Below him were two men of long service, ability and experience who were, perhaps, not sufficiently dynamic to produce powerful journalism. The job of head of a newsroom, whether in print journalism or broadcasting, is not an easy one and demands a fine balancing line between standing back and allowing junior journalists to have their head, and intervening too frequently. It seemed to me that it would be necessary to strengthen the news teams as speedily as possible by making new appointments, one at a higher level. There were difficulties, but I believe we reached satisfactory ways of determining their futures, and it was vital that we should have new blood near the top.

Below them, happily, there were some strong younger people. All they needed was more freedom and encouragement. Among those who moved up or took the chance for more vigorous work were George Sinclair as Head of Television News, Matt Spicer as Senior Producer in tv current affairs, and Geoffrey Cameron as Senior Producer in radio current affairs. Among others was James Cox, later well known to UK audiences, working in London, New York and elsewhere, but at that time with tv current affairs. He became our politics man when Chris Baur left. There was Tom Ross, who later went to Birmingham as the BBC's expert on motoring and car manufacturing. And among the youngest, then in their twenties, were Ken Cargill (now Head of TV News and Current Affairs) and Colin Cameron (now Head of Television in Scotland). There were other first-class people who ought to be named: John Milne, David Martin, George Reid, Mike Tosh, Iain Macwhirter and more. The talent was there. They seized the opportunity.

They were helped also by access to more money. That had been promised, and it was honoured for news, current affairs and features. It now also provided for the 'specialists' who were a most welcome extra to the programme makers. Michael Buerk was the first to come, dealing with the environment, energy and off-shore oil. When he went back south after two years he was replaced first, briefly, by Michael Cole (later the BBC's Court Correspondent and subsequently apologist for the Fayed brothers), and then by Mike Smartt, who did very well before he too went south. Chris Baur came some months later. He took a little time to adjust from his detailed reports for the *Financial Times* to the briefer requirements of broadcasting, but soon became a most welcome provider of perceptive reports, both short and long, for television and radio. He covered politics and some aspects of industry and was in heavy demand from London. As earlier noted, just before he went back to newspapers (*The Scotsman*), his one-hour *Power of Scotland* won the Royal Television Society's award for the UK's best documentary of 1978. He was replaced by James Cox, before he too went off to London.

Of the third specialist, Helen Liddell, the unjust ending of her short time with BBC Scotland has already been mentioned. Her intended post as 'economics reporter' was never given a proper chance. She would have been an excellent specialist, but her appointment was twice blocked from London. I was so angry and disappointed that I saw no point in seeking a replacement. Some time later, when Radio Scotland was about to become an all-day unit in the autumn of 1978, Peter Clarke was appointed—an amusing and mischievous man, always good to hear, but lacking Helen Liddell's wider economic knowlege.

As to the television programmes, the extra money and the additional staff from early 1976 all helped. Our main ones were the early evening *Reporting Scotland* five days a week, the weekly *Current Account* (early evenings, with 45 minutes of Scottish issues), and *Public Account* (also once a week, but more specifically focussed on politics, including the

Westminster parliament). In radio, there was *Good Morning Scotland*, at that time running for two hours, but today still going strong—or stronger, given its access to international affairs—and more recently for three hours each working day. *Twelve Noon* followed, a mixture of news and music; but until 1978 that was the limit of our extended news. Aberdeen ran its own *North Beat* five days a week (an irritation to Inverness, the Western Isles, and Orkney and Shetland, since it cut out the transmsitters from Central Scotland). In the evening, on VHF only, there was half an hour of Gaelic, which usually included about five or six minutes of news.

Much more of the news and related work follows later in this study. It covers the excellent work of tv's Current Affairs and documentary staff, the strengthening of radio in preparation for the November 1978 world-wide transmitter reorganisation, and other events such as the *Lilybank* affair (p 41). The great majority of this was good news. BBC Scotland came well out of it. So did our audiences.

Chapter 2

Transmitters, frequencies, and opt-outs'

Before going further, a brief look at how people in Scotland receive their television and radio. We have much for which to thank the engineers.

In 1975–6 what people saw on tv or heard on radio was mostly coming from England. And, worse, there were large areas of Scotland where the programmes were hard to receive at all. Central Scotland and most of the east and north-east coasts were fairly well covered by 625 television transmitters and by a variety of medium and VHF radio stations, together with Radio 2 on long wave, but even those areas still needed small relays to overcome high buildings or hills. This was true even in parts of Glasgow and Edinburgh, though extra relays were due soon. All 625 television work was planned and operated jointly by the BBC and ITV, with one or other looking after each mast.

But there were huge areas of the Highlands, the entire Western Isles, and extensive areas of southern Scotland which had only the old black-and-white transmitters and very poor reception on radio. In the south, 625 television existed only around Selkirk, Melrose and Galashiels, together with Berwick in the east and an area round Dumfries to the west—and Dumfries received only English news and programmes. Radio was better off, though there were still many gaps. Further west from Dumfries, only weak tv from England or from Northern Ireland was received. Closer to Stranraer, Belfast provided good reception. In the far north east, Caithness, Orkney and Shetland were well covered with new transmitters.

The most urgent need was to supply Lewis and Harris, together with the facing west coasts of the mainland. A huge mast was being built south of Stornoway, and another, not so large, on Mull, facing Oban. Plans for relays for Skye, Loch Ness, Fort William, Grantown and the upper Spey were all in hand. Nevertheless, quite understandably, a string of letters arrived at the BBC in Glasgow from Highland people who felt that they were being neglected. We had to maintain a steady flow of replies, providing the expected timetable for 625 transmitters and relays.

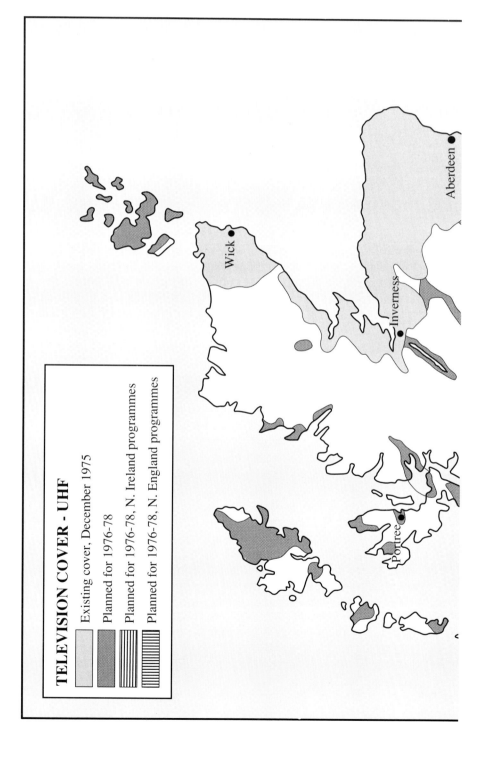

TELEVISION COVER - UHF

Existing cover, December 1975

Planned for 1976-78

Planned for 1976-78, N. Ireland programmes

Planned for 1976-78, N. England programmes

Wick

Aberdeen

Inverness

Portree

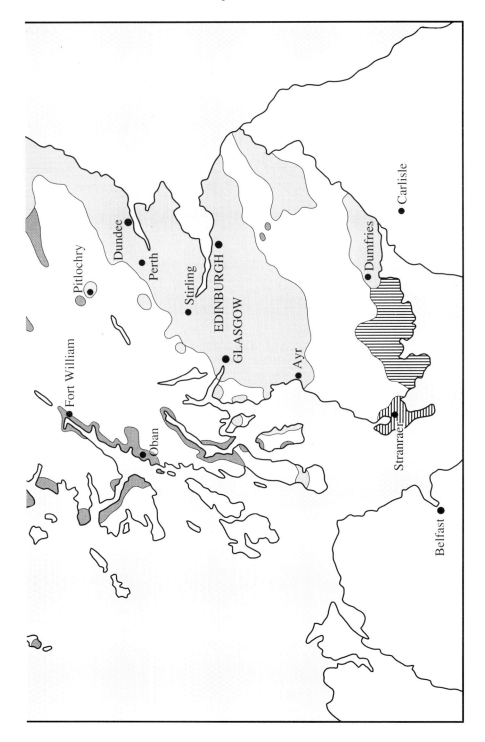

One such letter came to me from the well known and respected MP for the Western Isles, Donald Stewart. He knew that the huge Eitshal transmitter was under construction, but, he asked, would it be ready in time for the Olympic Games in June 1976? I was tempted to reply that the two BBC engineers from London who had been working on Eitshal while staying in Stornoway had been forced to leave the island that week. They had been observed working on that Sunday, because they wanted to complete the work in good time before the Games. They had been denounced from the Free Church pulpit in Stornoway that day, and their landlady had said that they must leave. No other landlady or hotel would take them, so on the Monday they had had to depart. My inclination was to reply to Donald Stewart that unfortunately, under the circumstances, the Western Isles would have to wait. But first I consulted our excellent Chief Engineer in Glasgow. 'No, no', he said: a Gaelic-speaking engineer with an aunt in Stornoway was already on his way north from Crystal Palace, and he would not think of working on Sundays in Lewis. So a promise—later fulfilled—was sent to Donald Stewart.

Another such affair came a year or so later. A relay was to be built south of Fort William, but the BBC in London, following standing rules, had refused a further link to Kinlochleven on the grounds that only if a village had more than 500 people could a relay be provided. The DG's office received a protest from an MP—either from Inverness or Argyll, I do not remember which—and the London office had drafted the usual explanation. Since the letter was to go to an MP, the draft letter was sent to me. At first I was mystified: surely Kinlochleven had more than 500 inhabitants? Then the point dawned: half of the town was north of the River Leven in the County of Inverness and half south of the river, in Argyllshire—a total of about 900 people. (Both halves are now in Inverness).

That afternoon there was a call from the engineers' office in London. One of their small construction units was finishing work at Pitlochry, so they planned to go on for a recce at Kinlochleven next day before going back to England in the afternoon. Did they know the distance, I asked? Yes, they had looked at the map: it was about 35 to 40 miles. On foot, perhaps, I said—but there is no road across Rannoch Moor. They had to go an extra 125 or more miles, but they did it willingly.

For *radio* the problems were quite different. In 1975–6 there was no real 'Radio Scotland'. For many years nearly all of the Scottish radio output was linked to the London-based Radio 4. Scotland was allowed to blot out London's Radio 4 for up to 33% of transmission time, but no more. This was known as 'opting out'. It was an irritation, both to people in Scotland who wanted to hear Radio 4 uninterrupted—

especially news, debates and Parliament—and no less of an annoyance to those Scots who wanted more news and comment from within Scotland. (The problem for television was similar, though it appeared to bring fewer complaints. But in 1975–6, for example, people watching tv north of the border received about 11% of Scottish origin. People in England received less than 1% of Scotland's tv output.)

The remedy for radio came from the International Telecommunication Union agreement in Geneva in October of 1975. After much bargaining, including almost all nations except North America, which made its own arrangements, frequencies were reallocated. This provided space for more programmes, though there was an increased risk of jamming at night in winter. The changes were not due to come into operation until 23 November 1978, but from that day Radio Scotland became a full-time unit with its own main frequency and lesser relays. It made the placing of Gaelic programmes easier, and also provided for separate news, discussion and music for Aberdeen, Inverness, Orkney, Shetland and the Western Isles.

All that had been planned during the Geneva negotiations and afterwards, and I was briefed about it soon after my arrival in the BBC. Much stress was placed on the transfer of Radio 4 from medium to long wave, with Scotland to be covered by strengthened transmitters at Westerglen (near Falkirk, in central Scotland) and at Burghhead, on the Moray Firth. This, I was told in London, meant that even if the Scottish Nationalists became dominant north of the Border, the BBC's Radio 4 would continue to broadcast to the whole of Scotland uninterrupted. When I was back in Glasgow I was quietly informed by a colleague that if a Scottish Assembly was set up and if the Scottish Government wanted a change, the two long wave transmitters could be altered within half an hour and other outlets given to Radio 4. 'If *you* give the instruction', I was told, 'we shall do it'. Interesting; but no such decision had to be made in my time.

High on the horizon and a worry to the BBC was the new Radio Clyde, which opened on 1 January 1974, created by James Gordon, a man of exceptional skill. Clyde had devised a mix of music, chat and news—and from the day it opened it won an audience in west and central Scotland that was much greater than any of the four BBC channels. Not until the autumn of 1978 was the new Radio Scotland launched, fresher and livelier than anything before. It no longer had to 'opt out' from someone else's programme, and, after an awkward start, Radio Scotland settled in and did well. Its launch had been delayed by the transmitter problems, but it eventually grew into a first-class operation, quite different in style from Radio Clyde, as reported in Chapter 9. Its real success came after my time.

Chapter 3

Drama, northern isles, and our network tv programmes

Drama is the most expensive of programmes and, after news, drama production was our other top priority. Alasdair Milne had set about building an output of plays that were both Scottish and acceptable to network controllers in London. Already short plays of a Scottish character were broadcast from Glasgow, as was the highly successful *Vital Spark* series. Gaelic, too, was getting more air time. The Queen Margaret Drive headquarters had a splendid studio, built to the same design as the finest in London, and the best outside London at that time. Milne's great success—for network—was the excellent Lewis Grassic Gibbon trilogy *A Scots Quair*, with *Sunset Song, Cloud Howe* and *Grey Granite*. They were first broadcast for BBC 2 in 1971–2 and were repeated with equal success ten years later.

Among the other successful plays that followed later, *Scotch on the Rocks* (1973–4) stood out—a hilarious semi-political affair, based on a book of which Douglas Hurd (more recently the Foreign Secretary) was co-author. Unfortunately objections from the SNP prevented a second showing on the grounds that it was damaging to the party, though no-one with a sense of humour would have taken it too literally. Memorable also, in 1974–5, not long before my move to Scotland, was *The Haggard Falcon*—a 16th century period serial set in the 'stews' of Edinburgh: a fast-moving, historically accurate thriller. It was one of the few films that I had a chance to see while still at *The Guardian*, and I had enjoyed it greatly.

At the same time, though, Scottish writers and producers in the BBC in London were working with distinction. Among these were Peter McDougall's *Just Another Saturday*, about Orange Marches in Glasgow (shot partly in Glasgow and partly in Edinburgh, the latter because Glasgow City Council was unhappy about it), but edited in the BBC's Ealing offices in London; and, no less memorably, John McGrath's *The Cheviot, The Stag and the Black, Black Oil*. These were the kind of programmes we hoped to make in Scotland.

Until 1976, and occasionally thereafter, there was also a system by which some of the Scottish staff, using our Glasgow studio A (which was fully up to London standards) 'hosted' programmes for London productions. The staff liked this, because it gave them greater experience and took them out on location for filming. One such, with a strong Scottish element, was *Sutherland's Law*, a series of 50-minute programmes based on the life of a North Argyll Procurator Fiscal (Iain Cuthbertson) and his wife (Edith Macarthur). It ran well from 1972 to 1976, with about twelve programmes each year. I rather hoped that we might take it over, since it was Scottish, but that was not achieved.

When I arrived in Glasgow there was no Head of Drama as such. Pharic Maclaren—a man of wide knowledge and charm, with an excellent reputation—was Senior Producer. Pharic had been the producer of *Sunset Song*, the first of the Grassic Gibbon series, and he also produced later (at the beginning of my time) Gibbon's *Clay*, *Smeddum* and *Greendon*, which was another outstanding success; but Milne, by now Director of Programmes in London, felt that because Pharic had to move in a wheelchair he was not fully fit to handle a wide range of programmes. It had therefore been agreed in London that, to strengthen drama, there should be a new appointment with the title Head of Drama. Three applicants were interviewed: two from BBC London, though with Scottish links, and Pharic. I had to chair the board, which was not easy; the majority vote went to Rod Graham, a Scot then at White City, who did very well in the following years. Nevertheless I felt very sad for Pharic, and uneasy in my own mind. Pharic was never quite the same, though he continued to work hard. Indeed, he had always tended to overwork. Sadly, he died young, about three years later.

The year 1975–6 saw a growth in BBC Scotland's drama output, initially under Pharic's control and later under Rod Graham. The growth would have been greater, but by then the Government was beginning to put a squeeze on BBC money. Fewer than half the proposals put forward by BBC Scotland were accepted in that year, or in the next two years. We were not unhappy, nevertheless, for despite the setbacks Scotland seemed to be making some progress.

Among those accepted for network in 1976–7 were *The Flight of the Heron*, a historical six-part story based on DK Broster's book, and another historical six-part series, *Rob Roy*, taken from the version (one of many) by Sir Walter Scott; in addition there were seven half-hour programmes for BBC's *Play for A* for BBC 2. These were low-cost but pleasing, with, among the titles, *Graffiti* (I cannot quite remember what it said, but I do remember that it was fun) and *To Glasgow, with Love*. And there was the return of Stevenson's *Weir of Hermiston*, which had been made for BBC 2 four years earlier. It was a friendly group, earning fair audiences. Even so, I hoped that we could include more contemporary drama. Our contributions from Scotland were, of course, in competition with such memorable serials as *I, Claudius*, with Derek Jacobi; *Sailor* (strictly speaking a documentary series about the Royal Navy, but with a dramatic element); Dennis Potter's *Double Dare*, and Peter McDougall's *The Elephant's Graveyard* (based in Greenock) using the massive resources of White City and Elstree.

For 1977–8, Rod Graham's first full year, there were disappointing rejections of Scottish proposals—mainly because of the Labour Government's further squeeze on BBC money. For BBC 1, Rod Graham saw his new 13-part drama *The Bloodletting* postponed at least to mid- or late-1978. A six-part adult thriller serial was cancelled. The six-part *Eagle of the Ninth*—the mystery of a Roman legion lost in the Scottish Highlands—went ahead, and was a great success. Three contemporary plays were reduced to two—one of the survivors being Sean McCarthy's *Thin End of the Wedge*, a clear success with exceptionally high audience figures. And Barrie's *What Every Woman Knows* went ahead, but for the following year.

For BBC 2, a six part life of Montrose was cancelled, but it would probably have been delayed in any case, as unfortunately the script was not ready. Stevenson's *Suicide Club*, a three part serial, was also delayed. Of three 75 minute plays, only one survived: Ibsen's *An Enemy of the People*. And of six thirty-minute plays, only three survived.

Later in the year, however, Rod was able to start work on *The Standard*, a contemporary series about life on a newspaper. The choice of newspapers was a slight embarrassment to me and I refrained from giving any advice, except for one point. One of the key characters was to be a woman, as chief sub-editor, and a senior man in London questioned whether that was likely. Since in my time at *The Guardian* I had appointed two women chief subs—both highly successful in their work—I said that there could be no objection. *The Standard* in its early stages looked good, but the audience figures were below average. So, under the pressures of that period, it died after its first thirteen episodes. In less tough times the series would probably have had a second chance. But, US style, it had none.

We had a little trouble, too, in that during that year we had in Scotland an overspend of some £400,000 for our drama department. That, however, was put right within weeks. Drama is expensive, with the combined costs of cast and crew, locations, studio sets and lighting, costume and make-up, uncertainties of weather and the reactions of actors. We managed to keep well within budget thereafter: Rod looked after that prudently.

The following year, 1978–9, brought another tough conflict to secure commissions from BBC 1 and BBC 2. Competition was so intense that our total of network drama was less than in the two previous years. London and Birmingham (Pebble Mill) did better. Still, we provided *What Every Woman Knows*, JM Barrie's tribute to women, which went well with audiences, as did John Buchan's *Huntingtower*. Also there was *The Slab Boys*, a beautiful Scottish contemporary play, full of humour, set in a steel workshop.

Our prime production of the year was the thriller *Running Blind*, a three-part story set at first in Scotland but mainly in Iceland. The story was dramatic enough in its own way, with manhunts and conflict set in remote landscape and on the wild Icelandic coast. But for the film crew and actors it was an equally dramatic experience—five or six weeks in wildly changing weather, with difficult roads, midges worse than in western Scotland (which is saying quite a lot), and exhaustion which led to one or two reinforcements having to be sent from Glasgow. But it produced good results. I wished that I had been able to go there myself for a day or two.

For the success of BBC Scotland's achievements in drama in those years I take no credit. Twice a year I had to put our case and explain our proposals to the Controllers of BBC 1 and BBC 2. I was well briefed, and argued our side with Rod Graham beside me. Alasdair Milne was also on our side, on the whole. It may be noted that, at least at that time, television did not often include dramas with a current political element. In my time, the outstanding and most forceful such programme was *Just Another Saturday*—mentioned a little earlier and the work of the three Scots based in London, Peter McDougall, John Mackenzie and Graeme McDonald. I wanted, if possible, to see more dramas in a contemporary setting being produced in Scotland. But I believe we moved in the right direction in those three years.

Orkney and Shetland

Soon after my BBC appointment was made public, Jo Grimond (MP, former leader of the Liberal Party) approached me. He was an old friend and on the *Guardian* board. He wanted me to spend a day or two in Orkney during the summer, as I often did. He wanted, however, above all, to persuade me of the need for two small radio stations, one each in Orkney and Shetland. They—the Orcadians and the Shetlanders—were fed up with having to listen to Aberdeen news, in which they had no interest, and hearing nothing of their own affairs.

Jo introduced me to a young farmer near Finstown who, on an exchange with a north Canadian young farmer, had worked part-time for a radio station over there with a staff of only two. If it could work in Canada, Jo said, it could work in the remoter parts of Scotland. I agreed. When I put it to Ian Trethowan, then Director of Radio, he said it could never work—but if I wanted to try it, he would help, though he was sure that it would die within a year. So we went ahead, with excellent help from the BBC's Glasgow engineers in putting together easy-to-handle equipment for the new staff. Offices were found in Kirkwall and Lerwick, each equipped to 'opt out' of Radio Scotland as required. The importance of these two stations was that each served an island group—some 18 occupied islands in Orkney and eight in Shetland, the latter stretching for over 70 miles south to north—and each had strong interests and a distinctive speech of its own. The islands urgently needed daily news about weather, fishing and farming conditions, shipping movements and information from their separate Island Councils.

Radio Orkney and Radio Shetland came on air in the spring of 1977. For each we had recruited and trained two broadcasters. As it turned out, three of the four were already living within their islands. In Orkney, Howie Firth was a mobile science teacher, based in Kirkwall but well known in all the Orcadian islands. In Shetland we took Jonathan Wills, no less well known as a vigorous journalist. (By coincidence, both had stood as candidates against Jo Grimond in the previous national elections: evidence, as Jo remarked with a mischievous smile, of the high calibre of competition against which he had won the seat.)

Each was backed by people with good experience in broadcasting— Liz Davis, from the Midlands, who had recently married an Orcadian, and Suzanne Gibbs, also from England but a frequent visitor to Shetland. They were strong teams, as we soon found, and their programmes were popular. Orkney's morning half hour reached the remarkable average of 70% of its people, and Shetland's early evening half hour achieved a similar level. Successful mid-day programmes were also run, some with music, and there were occasional debates. Each unit was backed by a secretary and a part-time assistant.

The success of these two small stations led to the founding of other small stations, not only in Scotland—one in Stornoway, mainly for Gaelic listeners, two in the Scottish Borders, Clwyd and Gwent in Wales, and Radio Foyle in Derry. The last succeeded in bringing together Catholics and Protestants, having won the respect of both.

Ian Trethowan had feared it could never work, but he had given us his blessing and the extra money and was among the first to salute our success. All those BBC small stations have earned a welcome and enthusiasm from their areas, and this has been made possible because they are linked to larger BBC units. The contrast with the recent failure of many of the small commercial stations is obvious.

Reports to the Staff and Public

Among the staff there was both concern and interest in what was happening, so I thought that I should talk to them. All those who wanted to come were invited to a meeting on July 27, 1976, just seven months after taking up my post in Scotland. I enjoyed this because there was a lot of good news to tell them. I intended to say nothing about the conflicts between myself, Curran, and others in London, and I kept to that.

Those who attended did so voluntarily. There was a good turnout in Glasgow. There were also radio links to Edinburgh, Aberdeen and Inverness. Questions could be asked in Glasgow, but not elsewhere, so I promised to visit each soon and answer their queries, if needed.

Meanwhile the main points to tell them were—

For Edinburgh, there was to be a new Broadcasting Centre on Leith Street at Greenside, with radio development to start the next year. For television, Edinburgh would be receiving new colour cameras by the following February.

For Aberdeen, I could promise increased demands on their studio and a second colour camera, and at least some likelihood of a new Radio Scotland frequency for their area.

And for Inverness, where our new Radio Highland had begun transmission only a few weeks earlier, all that I could say as yet was 'Very well done!'

As to Glasgow and BBC Scotland as a whole, there were three major points. First, we had been promised 'a big increase' in network television output. This was 'by far the most important thing' that had happened in the last six months. (It was before the Labour Government's cutback on BBC money). Second, we now had the prospect of major radio development, though most of that would come only in 1978. And, third, there was still the 'vexed question of devolution within the BBC' which 'should not be taken out of context'.

To extend these points, I said that in 1977 BBC Scotland would have the opportunity to 'double' its number of programmes for network BBC 1 and BBC 2—which meant more plays, more series, more documentaries, more light entertainment, more music and more arts programmes. But I also said that as we were still only at the 'offers' process all of it was therefore provisional and confirmation would not come

until the late autumn. The drama element now provided for ten network programmes and three local—for Scotland only. Looking beyond
that, we could look forward to a 13-part series, another six-part (50
minutes) thriller, and a third six-part 'family Sunday serial'. (In the
end, though, as already noted, the 13-part series was 'deferred', the
six-part thriller was scrapped, and only the six-part family serial went
ahead; but we were also given two single plays—and for BBC 2, three
plays by Scottish writers.)

In all, I spoke for almost 30 minutes, giving much time to the
expected radio developments two years ahead. Finally, and briefly, I
said that 'devolution within the BBC'—derived from what the Director-
General had said a year before—mattered, because by 1978 or 1979
'almost certainly Parliament will have created the Scottish Assembly'.
It was evident that we must be ready to show that BBC Scotland took
essentially Scottish decisions within Scotland; and we must be ready
to show to Parliament and to the Assembly 'that in everyone's interests
we ought to remain within the BBC system'.

And, at the end, I added, 'All of us, I believe, want BBC Scotland to
remain within the BBC family. We are not a family at war. We are a
family having a friendly discussion about how to overhaul our dom-
estic management. What matters, ultimately, is the quality of our
programmes'.

Only a few questions came at the end. So far as I could see, the
report had gone down well.

The second report was different. It was the BBC's Annual Report,
on 8 December 1976, in London, with Sir Michael Swann in the chair
and Sir Charles Curran doing most of the talking. There were radio
links to Glasgow, Cardiff and Belfast so that the press in each city could
ask questions after the main talk in the capital. Each of the three
Controllers had his own booth in Broadcasting House, but we had
strict instructions from Curran that we must answer only questions
about our own territories. It was, so far as I know, the first and last
such 'hook-up' for the Annual Report—though I believe that all three
of the Regional Controllers enjoyed it. Later the BBC series '*See For
Yourself*' gave individual viewers and listeners the chance to express
their views.

In Queen Margaret Drive ten newpaper journalists had turned up.
The first question came, appropriately, from the Press Association's
Jim Maguire, who wanted to know whether we could really expect
Scotland's network tv programmes to increase by one third. My answer
was that if taken in hours it would be more than one third. I listed
some of the programmes for the current year and others likely to
follow. The *Daily Record*'s John Calder followed up with the question

'Is Scotland getting a fair share?' He wanted to know whether we were getting a revenue 'proportionate to population'. My reply was that they had heard the DG saying that in the next two years 'the most significant part of development money' would be going to centres outside London, and that we were promised money in the next two years for the new Edinburgh centre, for the big increase in radio output. We must also welcome, I said, the opportunity we were to be given in network tv. As forecast, Scotland would do well.

The Scotsman and *Glasgow Herald* followed on, one on the costs of 90-minute drama and the other on Scottish expenditure within the UK average. The two most awkward questions followed from the *Scottish Daily Express* features man, Neville Garden (well known and much enjoyed later as presenter of *Good Morning Scotland*, *The Musical Garden* and now of *Queen Street Garden*). Why, he asked, was I prepared to stop at only one hour in 35 of UK network output coming from Scotland? And what would be the effect for Scotland of the 'cut-backs' of which the DG had spoken? I could only reply that, although Scotland had one in ten of the UK population, there were 'economic benefits' from making some programmes centrally, and that we wished 'to share in the heritage of BBC broadcasting'. But, I said, in future years we must hope for much more than one hour in 35 of network.

Further questions followed about the transmitters, giving me the chance to explain at length—with the long-wave Radio 4 masts due to come in 1978 near Falkirk and at Burghhead, the Sandale mast for Dumfries and Galloway, and extra extensions in the Highlands. I privately hoped that, a year later, I might have a stronger reply for Neville Garden. But I knew only too well that we would be lucky to get as much as one hour in 35 of tv network time. Our existing quota was about one hour in 50 for UK network. The Government cut-back on BBC money was hitting us, and the well established BBC units in London, Birmingham and elsewhere in England would fight hard to hold their output. We must just keep up our hopes.

(Network programmes, tv output 1975–6:

London	4802 hours
Other English	1079 hours
Scotland	141 hours
Wales	112 hours
N Ireland	14 hours)

(BBC Scotland, tv, Regional programmes

1975–6	397 hours
1976–7	435 hours
1977–8	450 hours
1978–9	416 hours)

Chapter 4

The Broadcasting Council for Scotland, the DG explodes, but better days come

So far the BCS (Broadcasting Council for Scotland) has had little mention. It was, though, of great importance to me. The National Governor for Scotland, a member of the BBC's Board of Governors, was automatically chairman of the BCS. My first chairman was Lady Avonside, wife of one of Scotland's senior judges. Lady Avonside was most energetic. Although she had tried twice to become a Conservative MP, she was strongly independent and a vigorous fighter for Scottish interests. One of the English Governors at that time said of her 'The trouble with Janet is that she does not know when she's won'. Having had a hand in supporting Sir Michael Swann's endeavour to get me back to Scotland, she most warmly welcomed my arrival. Indeed, before formally joining the BBC I attended four of the BCS's monthly meetings. I always got on well with her. Unfortunately, when I first met her she had only one year to go, and there was no chance of a Labour Government giving her a second term.

The Governors, strictly speaking, were appointed by the Queen. That had been established by the Royal Charter of 1927 and by the related Constitution. In practice, it was the Home Secretary and the Scottish and Welsh Secretaries who advised the Queen and made the decisions about appointments. The Governors met twice a month, mainly in London, but with regular visits to other BBC centres—in Scotland, on average, at least once in every three years.

The Scottish Governor, in turn, had a strong part in the appointment of BCS members. Those members are unpaid, apart from travel costs, and meet for a whole day once a month. They were chosen, in theory, by a small Scottish advisory council, composed of four or five worthy people, together with the Scottish Governor. The BBC Scotland Controller attended as an adviser. It was, and no doubt still is, a good BBC device. In my time it certainly brought in some admirable people who willingly gave of their valuable time. This was the line-up in my first year:

Lady Avonside, OBE (Chairman)

Major Allan Cameron, MBE, VL, JP, Vice Lord Lieutenant, Highland Region, farmer, landowner

Mrs Catherine Carmichael, Social worker and Senior lecturer, Glasgow University

Colin Carnie, Consulting Civil Engineer, partner in Crouch and Hogg, Glasgow

Dr Jennifer Carter, Senior Lecturer in History, Aberdeen University

Professor TA Dunn, Prof. of English and a founder member of Stirling University

Professor Sir Robert Grieve, First Chairman, HIDB; planner; mountaineer

Mrs Astrid Huggins, Lothian Regional Council (Conservative)

AH Kitson, Transport and General Workers' Union

Farquhar Macintosh, CBE, Rector, Royal High School, Edinburgh; Gaelic speaker, from Skye

The Rev James Ross, Minister of Paisley Abbey, Church of Scotland

James Young, Director, Ben Line shipping company. Worked in Edinburgh, lived in Stirlingshire

A term of three to five years was usual, and their reaction to our programmes and plans was of real value. One member was always asked to take part in the interviewing and appointment process for every senior post. Alasdair Milne had advised me to tell them as little as possible; I took the opposite line, and it was rewarding. Although critical at times, as they should be, in general the BCS gave me splendid support.

Among those who came in later in my time were Mrs Helen Davidson, an SNP supporter from Stirling; Mrs Elwena Fraser, executive, Perth Festival of the Arts; Sir Norman Graham, former Secretary to the Scottish Education Department; and Mr Duncan McPherson, farmer on the Black Isle and a Highland Regional Councillor—latterly its Convenor. The invitation to Mrs Davidson followed my suggestion to both the BCS and to the advisory group that, since we had members who were open supporters of the Conservatives, Labour and the Liberals, it was odd that the Council had never had a known Nationalist. After taking advice, I met Mrs Davidson; she was willing to serve, and she was accepted by all the others. She turned out to be a valuable member—so much so that, long after I had gone, she was retained on the small advisory council. Her husband had been a BBC engineer, and she cared a lot about the BBC.

Discussion as to the governor to follow Lady Avonside in May of

1976 had formed part of my meeting with the Secretary of State, William Ross, in October 1975. Unknown to the other, each of us had come to the meeting with a list of possibilities, and uncannily the two lists had much in common. Three names were on both lists—Sir Norman Graham, newly retired from the Scottish Office (but Ross said that he might be needed for something else); Professor Dunn, of Stirling University, who was already a member of the BCS; and Professor Nisbet, Professor of Education at Aberdeen University. Either of the first two I would have welcomed; of the third I knew less, but he was certainly a possibility. Last on Ross's list was Professor Alan Thompson, former Labour MP for Dunfermline and lately Professor of the Economics of Government at Heriot-Watt—a fine title. Almost as an afterthought, Ross said he 'must find something' for Thompson after his time as a Labour MP—and in the end Alan Thompson it was. (Why Sir Norman Graham was held back I never knew: he would have been ideal, and he later served the BBC well as a BCS member from early 1978.)

Because of his university work, Alan Thompson was unable to give the BBC as much of his time as Lady Avonside had done. His commitment as a governor meant spending about two days every fortnight in London or elsewhere, with the typical BBC heavy load of documents to study, and in addition he had to chair the BCS once a month. It soon became clear that he was chiefly interested in the UK aspects of his new appointment, rather than the Scottish side. Nevertheless, such minutes of the governors' meetings as I saw (only matters directly related to BBC Scotland) showed him trying manfully to stand up for Scottish interests, but more often than not being battered down by such tough characters as Mark Bonham-Carter (Vice-Chairman) and Roy Fuller (a solicitor and Oxford's Professor of Poetry). They had previously enjoyed conflicts with Lady Avonside; Alan Thompson did not have her vigour and commitment to fight to the last.

It was over the BCS that I had my next conflict with the Director General. On the evening of 6 January 1977, Charles Curran rang me to say that, the night before, he had been 'in a rage' over a paper that I had written for the December meeting of the BCS—a paper which he said I should not have written or given to the Council—and, he declared, he was still 'exceedingly cross'. (As Huw Wheldon's biographer, Paul Ferris, says, Curran was 'a choleric man'.) He had put the matter before the Governors that day. He accused me of using the BCS 'in a most improper way'. He did not mention, though he must have known, that the Council had given me its full support at its December meeting.

The origin of my paper for the December meeting went back to the late summer of 1976. In an informal private talk in Edinburgh, Sir Michael Swann had surprised me by saying that a 'directorate' for Scotland was not impossible. He believed that there was 'broad sympathy' among the governors for what we were trying to achieve through 'mini-devolution'. Because the DG was so strongly against any 'directorate' when we had talked before I joined the BBC, I had never pressed the matter, but apparently Swann now thought that Curran might be more amenable. In November, therefore, I had prepared a paper to put before the BCS. I had sent a copy privately to Sir Michael; he had made no comment, one way or other. My great mistake was in not sending a copy to Charles Curran before I sent it to BCS members—though in the end the result would have been much the same.

In essence, my proposal was this. BBC Scotland would become a directorate, headed by Director Scotland instead of Controller Scotland. It would have its own capital and operation budgets, agreed annually, but still subject to some central (London) procedures. If the BBC centrally agreed to a division into major, major-minor, and minor items, BBC Scotland would have an annual allocation to cover its major-minor and minor items. In general, major items would include irregular requirements costing more than, say, £75,000 each (by 1976 levels). New television studios or new broadcasting centres or new Outside Broadcasting units would come within that. My outline went on to the likely items of the major-minor and minor items; and it covered engineering standards, central purchasing by the BBC, and other matters. The Director Scotland should have the right to attend Board of Management meetings, but should do so only when relevant (Scottish) matters were to be discussed. I was determined that somehow the absurd system by which I could be called to London twice, or sometimes three times, in a week must be stopped.

As to the television network programmes, I proposed that the present system of 'programme offers' by Scotland, as by London and Birmingham, to the Controllers of BBC 1 and BBC 2 should continue. The full cash cost of each programme and the agreed 'variables' (costumes, lighting, design etc) would be repaid to BBC Scotland. But I put forward, for later agreement, a system by which programmes could be made in Scotland—and abroad—for sale to BBC 1 or 2 after completion. (The current sum allowed to Scotland each year for self-generated programmes was then no more than £10,000.)

All this had been put before the Broadcasting Council for Scotland in December. They had had my paper some days before. There was questioning and discussion. Overall, and without objections, my paper was warmly accepted. The minutes had gone, among others, to the Director General. He had apparently not read them until after New Year—indeed not until the day before the Governors' meeting on 6 January. Hence his explosion. As I read later from the minutes, he told the governors that I had known 'for at least a year' that he (Curran) was wholly opposed to any form of a directorate. In his view the Board of Managers came together simply 'to help the DG run the BBC'. The regions were *not* ultimately in control of their affairs in their own right. A directorate based in Scotland would, on the strictly centralist interpretation, have infringed upon the BBC's capacity to make decisions. Moreover, the BCS, he thought, was quite 'irrelevant' to any managerial process.

Professor Thompson—to his great credit, in my view—said that the minutes of the BCS's December meeting 'actually reflected the strength of the Council's support for the idea of a Scottish Directorate'. Two governors spoke in criticism of my action; two others suggested caution, because of the possible reaction in Scotland.

Curran's hostility puzzled me at the time. He had less than three months to go before retirement—Swann having nudged him into going early, to let Ian Trethowan take over. Curran had nothing to gain by his storm. But, thinking about it later, it seemed probable that being edged out may have aggravated his anger.

With hindsight, there is a strong case for saying that Curran should never have become Director General. His appointment happened in 1967, after Charles Hill—at one time a notable MP and then Chairman of the ITA—became the BBC's chairman. It was a unique event, brought about by Harold Wilson as Prime Minister. Wilson, it was thought, wanted to 'humiliate' the BBC and he saw Hill as the man to do it. At first Hill had as Director General the highly forceful Hugh Carleton Greene, who had already spent over ten years in the post. Green retired in 1969, some believing that he was, in effect, forced out by Hill's appointment. The obvious man to take over was Huw Wheldon (later Sir Huw), at that time Managing Director of Television— another man of great strength and originality. However Hill, for his own reasons, wanted someone less dominant and he seems to have persuaded the governors to choose Curran, at that time Director of External Broadcasting: in my view a bad mistake.

On 12 January, in the week after the Governor's meeting, at the DG's wish we had a private talk in his room in Broadcasting House. The atmosphere was quite different to his angry mood on the sixth. The 'Directorate' was mentioned only once, at the start, and was then set aside. Curran preferred to begin by discussing my troubles in trying to move staff from one post to another. I saw this as essential to the strengthening of news and current affairs, but BBC rules prevented it. He promised, in effect, further help from the Director of Personnel. (This followed a year of efforts on my part.) We went on to discuss the concern of the BCS over Scotland's share of UK network programme making, on which I said that, in spite of all the promises, Scotland looked like getting fewer network commissions than in the previous year. The DG said that money was tight because of Government restrictions, which was true.

Then, his final main point, he said that 'senior colleagues' saw my handling of the BCS as 'either naive or mischievous'. He hoped that it was neither. My reply was that he and his colleagues must take account of the time limit against which we were working—the probable arrival of the Scottish Assembly in early 1978. Senior staff in London seemed unwilling to consider this. So far, both the Broadcasting Council and I had wanted to retain BBC Scotland under the BBC's umbrella. It was not our wish to promote separation. The DG agreed to consider this. It was also agreed that we must all wait for the Annan Report, due in February; and a week or two later it was agreed that Sir Michael Swann and the DG would attend the March meeting of the BCS: of that, more comes later.

'Devolution' and 10 Downing Street

While the DG's colleagues may have thought little of the possiblity of Scottish and Welsh 'Assemblies', the Prime Minister saw them as of prime importance. James Callaghan had moved into Downing Street in April of 1976, after Harold Wilson's retirement, and in the next few months the new PM was deeply involved in the fight against inflation, together with European and international affairs. But in November the Queen's Speech gave a high place to devolution for Scotland and Wales. The second reading of the Bill went through the Commons in mid-December, with thirty working days set for it. Meanwhile the Conservatives had countered with the lesser plan of a 'Scottish Convention' with limited powers.

But there were conflicts, both within and outwith the Labour Party. On February 22, the day of the guillotine debate, the Chief Whip told the PM that the vote would probably be lost by about thirty. The actual number was 29. The eleven Scottish National Party members had voted against (because in their view the terms were inadequate); two Labour MPs had left the party in protest against slow progress; and ten Labour members had voted against the Government, while a further 29 had abstained. On the other side, five had voted for the Bill, while 28 abstained.

In mid-March the Government had another serious loss, over the public expenditure plans for 1977–8. The next day Mrs Thatcher tabled a 'No Confidence' motion for the following week. That galvanised the Prime Minister to embark upon a series of confidential discussions with, separately, David Steel for the Liberals and James Molyneaux for the the Ulster Unionists. (For a fascinating account of that and further events, see James Callaghan's book *Time and Chance*, pp 449 to 460 and 504 to 507.) By the morning of the 'No Confidence' debate, Callaghan was able to tell his Cabinet what he had done and to win their approval. That night Mrs Thatcher's motion was rejected by 322 votes to 298. The 13 Liberals voted with the Government, while the Ulster Unionists divided, some for and some against. The Scottish Nationalists and Plaid Cymru voted with the Conservatives.

All this, of course, had a direct relevance to my troubles with the BBC's Director General, even though he was in his last weeks of authority. A Scottish Assembly was very much a live issue, and BBC Scotland—and the BBC in London—had no real alternative but to take it into account. In a short written agreement between the Prime Minister for the Government and David Steel for the Liberals, it was stated that 'legislation for devolution' must progress. Steel had suggested 'a fresh start', with separate terms for Wales and Scotland, and Callaghan had agreed. There was no doubt about the Government's intentions. The Assembly was coming. Then, as now, the BBC had some of Britain's best political and parliamentary journalists. Had Curran and his friends heard or watched their own programmes, they would have known much more about Scottish affairs.

The Assembly also had implications for BBC Scotland's finance and the involvement of the Home Office. Three times in 1975 and early 76, the Secretary of State for Scotland, William Ross, had had private talks with me—once at his request and twice by mine. At each of the three meetings he mentioned the possibility that the Assembly might want to take over from the Home Office the ultimate control of broadcasting in Scotland. At least, he said, it would want an annual report and debate. This I had relayed to Charles Curran and others in London. I said that we must be prepared for it. (It was not the first time that I had said that.)

Swann, as usual, took more note than Curran. But it also, indirectly, led me into a small difficulty with the Director of Finance, Paul Hughes, one of the most friendly of people except when you questioned his decisions. My problem was that although in Scotland we had secured more money for 1975–6 and for the next year—for which we were very grateful—I believed that we were not getting all that we should. A careful look at the BBC's annual *Handbook*, a most useful document, led me to this conclusion. Its 'analysis' of costs seemed to imply that an excessive sum was being demanded from us for transmitting UK programmes (other than those we made and sold to the networks, BBC1 and BBC2). I took it up with Hughes. He did not like my questions. It seemed that it was left to lesser staff in London to determine what we must pay. No clear answer ever came.

At the time, the BBC was selling many UK programmes to RTE in Dublin, including some of ours from Scotland. RTE was paying only a small fee, because the BBC thought that RTE2 could not manage without this benefit. But in effect we were having to pay London a much higher sum. It was galling. Whether because of my questions or for other reasons, from 1978 onwards no details of charges were included in the Handbook. The 'analysis' had gone. A loss.

(For figures, see Appendix 2)

Swann's friendly warning to the BCS

James Callaghan, as Prime Minister, had outflanked Mrs Thatcher, the new Leader of the Opposition. Sir Michael Swann outflanked Sir Charles Curran. On 12 January 1977 Curran had said that he would come to the March meeting of the Broadcasting Council for Scotland, together with Swann if possible. Instead, Sir Michael came alone to the February meeting. It was one of the most interesting in all my time with BBC Scotland.

Sir Michael took the chair himself, instead of Professor Thompson. The first item was a paper written by me immediately after the mid-January talk with the DG. It was titled 'BCS objectives'. I had sent a copy to the DG before sending it to BCS members on 20 January. It began by recalling the objectives of the BCS, as set out for the Annan Committee *before* I joined the BBC. (The BCS chairman then was Lady Avonside.) The three objectives were these:

1) More effective influence and participation by BBC Scotland in central decision making;
2) More autonomy in management and financial matters;
3) More programme-making both for network and for Scotland.

Further, on behalf of the BCS, Lady Avonside had said that the proposed 'mini-devolution' was a transfer of authority, and she wanted a Scottish seat on the Board of Management for the Controller or Director.

In my paper I wrote that, as members might remember, I had initially had reservations about the proposed 'mini-devolution'. However, after some experience within the BBC—and especially of its highly centralised nature—I had suggested a 'directorate' as a mid-way compromise. That would have given the senior Scottish executive the right to attend Board of Management meetings in London, but they would only do so when necessary. That, however, had been unacceptable to the DG. (Ironically, looking ahead, one of the first things Ian Trethowan did on becoming DG was to make the Head of News and Current Affairs in London a Deputy Director, with much the same freedom of attendance.)

My paper then went on to the aspects of management and finance. At the time of my appointment I had understood from both the chairman (Swann) and the Director General that substantial moves were to be made towards greater autonomy for BBC Scotland. Without that, I said, I would not have taken the job.

At the start of the Broadcasting Council meeting on that February day, Sir Michael invited comments on the question of management and finance. He said also that there was no question of London 'foisting' candidates on Scotland (the new Head of Drama had recently been appointed, with Pharic Maclaren failing to secure the post). In effect, Swann said, there were two rights of veto—one from Scotland and one from London. This brought a vigorous reply from Mr Farquhar Macintosh, Rector of the Royal High School in Edinburgh, and originally from the Isle of Skye. The central authorities in London, he said, 'ought to be more conscious of coming political events'. That ought to apply, he said, whether or not the Scottish and Welsh Bill went through in its present form. He also thought that the present BBC system was too time-consuming and inefficient. The constant requirement to refer to London undermined the authority of the Scottish management. Mrs Carmichael (Glasgow and politically towards the left) and Mrs Huggins (Edinburgh and towards the right) spoke in similar terms. I was grateful to all three. Sir Michael said that while he might perhaps not go as far as Mr Macintosh wanted, he was convinced that devolution must come. It was clear that the BCS members were in sympathy with what Mr Macintosh had said.

The discussion moved on to the controversy over the post of Editor, News and Current Affairs, to take the place temporarily undertaken by Andrew Boyle. My view had been that the post must go to someone of the BBC's higher 'MP7' grade or the 'A' level above it. (At that time, apart from myself, BBC Scotland had only one man at 'A' level and only two at 'MP7') The chairman explained that within the 'MP7' grade there was flexibility. That was the level at which I should look. In London the News and Current Affairs staff had only six people of 'A' level. Sir Michael was confident that if I talked to the right people I could get the kind of quality that I wanted. I was less confident, after other problems, but it seemed worth another try.

Next, the Government's pay policy: the BBC had suffered from it. Sir Michael said that although the weekly staff had received some increase, the monthly staff had received nothing. (This, it may be remarked, was when inflation was at about its worst, 28% or thereabouts). As a result, BBC salaries were 20% or more below ITN levels. But whatever the newspapers might be doing to overcome the pay freeze—and they had found their own ways— the BBC could not employ a 'fiddling' of its grades.

Sir Robert Grieve, former founding chairman of the Highlands and Islands Development Board, said that central (London) authorities should take account of the atmosphere being generated in Scotland. The Scottish management must be seen to have greater freedom of manoeuvre. Sir Michael said that there was already flexibility. I then suggested that, to provide for more freedom for the Scottish management without taking away the needs of the central authorities, there could be mutual prior approval of a short list. That should include agreement on the salary range to be offered before any appointment. When that was agreed, I said, decisions should be left to Scotland (and Wales if wished) without further reference to London. Representatives from London would of course be welcome to attend at appointment boards. The chairman cautiously replied that he would like to see that in writing. (It would have been a good step forward for us, but it never happened.)

There were further exchanges, with Mr Macintosh and Sir Robert Grieve both saying that the system was too rigid, that there were too many points of friction between Scotland and the centre, and that there were too few opportunities for Scottish influence at the top. Mrs Carmichael questioned the basis of comparison between Scotland and London. BBC Scotland, she said, was having to pull itself up by its bootstraps and must be allowed to make its own mistakes. Mr James Young wanted better information from London. The chairman hoped that that would come. He reminded the BCS of the money provided for the Inverness development and for Orkney and Shetland. While staff in London had been reduced, Scotland had grown. The Rev James Ross said that while glad of the recent favourable treatment they were 'unrepentant' about making a fuss. The recent benefits, he said, had been due to Scotland, because of past neglect.

What I have reported from that morning's exchanges is no more than an outline. Sir Michael went on to list a number of changes now planned for Scotland—not major, but welcome. There were further comments from BCS members. Finally, the chairman said that 'the Scottish turbulence' had had 'an essentially hopeful aspect.' A lot had been achieved in the past year. (In a friendly report to the governors

at their next meeting, Sir Michael said that Scottish Broadcasting
Council members had treated him 'in a somewhat Olympian manner',
like headmasters dealing with a wayward pupil; but it had been a
constructive day.)

It was a good day in my view also. The Broadcasting Council mem-
bers had stuck to their demand for a stronger BBC Scotland and the
BBC's chairman had responded with respect for Scottish needs. Soon
Ian Trethowan would take over as DG. There was hope for better days.
But the Helen Liddell disaster was soon to come.

Annan, money—and plans for BBC Scotland's growth

A little late, the Annan Report was published on March 24, 1977.
That day we had another 'report to the staff' for BBC Scotland, relaying
it from Queen Margaret Drive to Edinburgh, Aberdeen and Inverness.
But before starting on Annan, I took the chance to send birthday
greetings to BBC Highland which had begun broadcasting exactly
one year before. They had done admirably, in Gaelic as in other
programmes. (Its manager was William Carrocher, new to the BBC.
He was an Ayrshire man who had worked as a journalist in the
Western Isles, where he taught himself Gaelic. He had then gone into
the foreign service, at one point serving in the Far East, and had
returned to Scotland as a freelance broadcaster, among other things.
He was noted for his mischievous style, and his *Ceilidh air Carrocher*
programme, a mix of Gaelic and English, was taken for all of Scotland.)

As to Annan, it was a good report. Yes, there were some sharp
criticisms, but overall it was welcome equally to us in Scotland and to
the whole BBC. I ran through a summary.

For BBC Scotland:
—It said that we should be making more UK network programmes (which was exactly what we wanted to do)
—It said, in effect, that we should have greater financial and
   management control of our own affairs (just what our Broadcasting Council had proposed)
—It said that we should control our own scheduling for BBC1
   (instead of having to get clearance from London) but should
   leave BBC2 as an entirely UK channel
—And, on transmitters, it gave the highest priority to completing
   the 625 tv system in Northern Scotland and the Western Isles
   (as we wished).

All this, of course, depended on Government approval. Looking back from 1992 to 1977, I wonder whether I ought to have warned our Scottish staff that there might be trouble with London over finance and management—as I knew there would be, since there already had been.

For the BBC as a whole, Annan recommended that the BBC's Charter should be extended from 1979 to 1994. BBC Radio, a majority of the Annan Committee said, should *not* be separated from BBC Television: it was thought that by staying together they would save money and assist in withstanding outside pressures. But they proposed that the BBC should transfer all its local radio to a new authority. (This was by far the biggest worry to the BBC in London, with some 30 local radio stations then and 20 more to come; rightly, the BBC from 1977 onwards strongly opposed any such move, not least because of the valuable interchange of news between local radio and the BBC's four network radios and its BBC1 and BBC2 tv). The Annan Committee also said that the separation should apply to Wales and Scotland, but since neither had any self-contained local stations, nor any such plans, that did not apply.

There were many other proposals in the Annan Report, both for the UK as a whole and for Scotland. That day I went on to give the staff a more detailed account of the Annan recommendations for Scotland. If accepted by the Government they meant faster completion of the transmitters, more network programmes from Scotland (and Wales and Northern Ireland), more direct control of scheduling of Scotland's BBC1 but no 'opting out' on BBC 2, and increased Gaelic programmes on radio and tv, mainly from Inverness. It meant, too, more output from Aberdeen.

We had, in fact, already prepared to double the Gaelic output from Inverness in April. Less welcome was Annan's view that the Orkney and Shetland mini-stations—due to open in May—should eventually be transferred to a new local broadcasting authority. (Since that authority was never created, Orkney and Shetland have remained as valuable BBC units, with the Western Isles and the two Borders stations added later.)

One other point: the Annan Committee said that BBC Scotland should remain as part of the BBC and should not be transferred to a Scottish Assembly. Annan was concerned lest our editorial independence might be 'undermined'. We were to provide the Assembly with an annual report, as we did to Parliament, and our Broadcasting Council should 'take account' of what the Assembly might say. That had been my view when talking to Noel Annan and Sir James Mackay a year earlier. Now, in March of 1977, my view was changing. Though I said nothing to the staff, after the way I had been treated by Curran and some of his London associates I would have been ready now at least to review my personal standing.

Finally, the Annan Report had mentioned 'a widespread feeling' in Scotland that output from both BBC Scotland and Scottish Television were 'mediocre' in quality. That seemed to me an unjust judgment, perhaps partly because most of the Committee's evidence had been drawn from 1974–5. Even at that, *Sunset Song, Clay-Smeddum, Scotch on the Rocks, The Haggard Falcon,* a whole range of light entertainment network, *The Sounds of Scotland,* the Anne Lorne Gillies series, the coverage of the Edinburgh International Festival, the work of our two orchestras, the religious broadcasts of exceptional skill, *Public Account* and *Current Account, Good Morning Scotland*; these and many others were far above being mediocre.

All the same, I said, the Annan Report was in general good for us. There was much to encourage BBC Scotland and its staffs.

Having talked about Annan, I took the chance also to talk about two more matters—the licence fee, fixed by the Government, and then our own Scottish development plans. But before going on I said that anyone who had had enough was of course free to leave. I had been surprised by the number who had turned up—all voluntarily, and at risk of missing their mid-morning coffee or early lunch—but nearly all stayed for more.

The licence fee was, of course, almost the only source of money for the BBC. The Labour Government was now planning an annual settlement, instead of the three-year system. It was important to explain our position to the public whenever possible. We had the lowest fees in Europe—colour £18 a year, black and white £8. The Republic of Ireland was next lowest, at £27 for colour and £18 for black and white. Germany next, demanded £28 for either. (In Britain in early 1992, the fee is £80 for colour.)

The point of emphasising the figures was so that our staff could remind friends and others of how much they were getting at a very low cost. As a further example of BBC good management, BBC studios were averaging 18 minutes a day of finished major programmes (drama and such), while Finland was next at 16 minutes, the Netherlands 14 minutes, and then France and Spain at 11 minutes. West Germany and Italy, commonly thought to be the most efficient, were getting only five minutes of completed programmes from each studio. Not bad, in a competitive world. The ITV companies, of course, spent much more money on comparable programmes—and, under trade union pressure, they paid staff at higher levels than the BBC.

Finally, BBC Scotland's development plans. You might wonder, given all the pressures already mentioned, how we could find money for developments. But our plans were taking shape—and this, I know, was the part of that morning's discussion of greatest interest to the staff. We had many reasons to be grateful for the hard work of Brendan Slamin, borrowed from his post as BBC Scotland's Head of Engineering to act as Head of Development. He was a wonderful man—cheerful, constructive, full of ideas, and always ready to criticise in a friendly way what I was saying or doing. His outline brought good news for Edinburgh, Glasgow, and Aberdeen and above all for the new Radio Scotland, which was to be in operation all day and in the evenings from the late autumn of 1978.

There was to be a new building in Edinburgh, six minutes' walk from the Scottish Assembly, which was being prepared at the old Royal High School. It would be convenient for interviews and discussion with Assembly members, with studios for television and radio, but the new building's main use would be as headquarters of the new Radio Scotland. That building could not be ready before the autumn of 1981, but plans were being prepared. (The plan was abandoned after the Assembly was voted out by the Commons in the spring of 1979, but there were already doubts within the BBC about the building, both because of costs and because the Scottish Symphony Orchestra was reluctant to move from Glasgow to Edinburgh.)

For Glasgow, there was to be an enlarged tv Studio B, and there was still hope, though not in the existing year, of the higher level of television drama. Aberdeen was to get more radio staff, and Dundee was to have a full-time journalist.

Such were the expectations in March of 1977, and apart from the new Edinburgh building most of it was carried through. In place of the new building, there was extensive renovation and improvement of the old Queen Street headquarters, though it was to be ten years or more before that work was completed.

A warm welcome to DG Ian Trethowan

This is worthy of a section of its own, simply because Ian Trethowan was such a relief after Charles Curran. He had hoped to come up to us in May, but other work delayed his visit until the Broadcasting Council's July meeting. He began by speaking about the BBC's finances. They were in the red due to ever-rising costs, but the government was reluctant to give us any help. Added to this, 'phase three' of the Government's incomes policy, aimed at curbing inflation by holding down pay increases, meant that we were unable to offer competitive salaries. As a result, staff were leaving to go to commercial companies. Bryan Cowgill (Controller of BBC1, tv) had just been lost to Thames.

Trethowan went on to say that, in accordance with a wide feeling among staff, the BBC's administration must be simplified. Annan had referred to the 'bureaucratic fog' of the BBC, and that must be put right. Michael Checkland (Controller Planning) was working on that. He went on to praise the improvement in journalism in the BBC, with a special word about my own work in BBC Scotland—and on this he hoped that I might help with advice in the centre. (He had been a journalist himself for many years before going to ITN and then to the BBC, and he had a warm feeling for journalism.)

He went on to answer a long list of questions from members of the Broadcasting Council, waiting each time to hear the member's view fully before responding. One slight surprise came from Mrs Davidson, our first Scottish National Party member, who said that speaking for herself she did not want to see BBC Scotland separated from the Corporation. At the same time, she believed that BBC people in London needed to change their attitude to BBC Scotland; but, overall, she had 'a strong affection' for the BBC. That went well with our new DG, and he went well with us.

After lunch some of us took him for a walk through the Botanic Gardens, across the road from Broadcasting House. It was a beautiful sunny day, and he particularly admired the whitebeams, then at their best. His next visit came in November, and that went very well too.

Chapter 5

Lilybank

The east end of Glasgow contained some rough and deprived areas—
though with many decent people who wanted better lives for themselves and for their children. These problems had largely been
ignored—BBC Scotland and Scottish Television had rarely made programmes about the east end, apart from visits to Celtic Football Ground
and Beardsmore's big workshops. Having been brought up on the west
side of the city, in the comfortable surroundings of Hillhead, I had seen
little of it, but it seemed essential to bring it to public attention. How
could we find a sensitive approach?

The answer came through one of our Broadcasting Council
members, Mrs Catherine Carmichael. As a child she had been brought
up in the east end of Glasgow. Now she was a Senior Lecturer in Social
Work and Social Administration at Glasgow University, and she was
deputy chairman of the (UK) Supplementary Benefits Commission.
From 1974 to 76 she had also been a part-time member of one of
Prime Minister Wilson's 'think tanks' at 10 Downing Street. What we
did not know until long afterwards was that for ten weeks in the early
winter of 1976 Mrs Carmichael, under a different name, had lived in
a poor local authority flat in Parkhead. She was on leave from the
university, and believed to be abroad. To experience and understand
what life in such circumstances was really like, she had lived strictly
on the social security level of £10.50 a week.

Not far from where she was living, in a group of streets which were
due for renovation, a group of tenants were getting together to try to
improve their environment. They had established the *Lilybank Tenants'
Association*, and they had harried the council's Housing Department,
eventually persuading them to revise their methods (at no extra cost).
Their 1930s houses had been quite well built, but were suffering
severely from vandalism, degradation and the effects of a rather violent
community. But this was a vigorous group. In *Lilybank Tenants' Association* there was a determined and purposeful group of citizens—just
what we needed for a constructive documentary.

My role was simply to get the programme going. Matt Spicer, as

Head of Current Affairs and Documentaries, was supervisor. As producer, David Martin did the bulk of the work. (He later became Senior Producer, Features.) He began filming just after New Year 1977, to secure pictures before the major work began. Thereafter further filming continued until the end of the summer. Magnus Magnusson came in as the questioner and presenter. Some people thought he was too Edinburgh-and-Oxford-orientated for the job, but he was cool and level in his questioning, which was the right approach. Once they understood what we were trying to do, the *Lilybank* people were enthusiastic, though one or two did not want to appear on screen.

In the editing, four units were made—three of 45 minutes each for Scotland, and one for UK network, at one hour, if accepted. Of the three, the first was about the campaign raised by the tenants' association and reactions to it, then one about the rebuilding of the houses and the influence of the association, and the third was a public meeting with Magnus Magnusson raising questions and taking comments: a bit boring, you might think—but not to those who eventually saw it.

The cost of the programmes was small, since the performers were free (though we gave the association some money afterwards). Within the programmes there were some strong shots of children playing in the stone and mud of derelict land, some of whom ought to have been at school. Among ourselves there was some debate as to whether their language would be understood by English audiences—replies to questions about why they were not at school, among other things, and among the boys on why they were preparing to fight their rivals on the other side of the main road.

So far as we could discover, no such programme had ever been made within Scotland—certainly not by BBC Scotland, Scottish Television or Grampian. The only near equivalent was the work of Granada, who had had two men in Dundee for nearly a year in 1975–6, working on corruption in the local council. That programme caused a stir when broadcast on ITV network, with three councillors being subsequently prosecuted.

Our programmes were ready in the late autumn, after completing the filming of public reactions. Alasdair Milne then saw the one-hour version and did not like it. But we then had an unexpected bonus. The BBC's governors came to Glasgow at the beginning of November—the only occasion, in my period, when they all came together for the best part of two days. Their main business was completed in private session, at Queen Margaret Drive, on the morning of November 3. They then had lunch with the senior Scottish staff, and for the afternoon I had been instructed to show them some of our recent work.

I had five tapes ready—one drama, one light entertainment, two others, and the one-hour *Lilybank*. Sir Michael Swann had, with apologies, gone through to Edinburgh after lunch, and the chair was taken by George Howard (of Castle Howard, better known to most of us later as Brideshead of the Granada series). I explained what the five programmes were: Howard said 'Give us the one you'd most like us to see'. I played *Lilybank*.

At the end, with the lights up, there was total silence. Then the bulky Howard got out of his front row seat, turned round to the rest of the governors and BBC staff from London, and said something (as I remember) like this: 'That was fascinating, excellent, something that was good for us all to see'. I was, of course, absolutely delighted.

Afterwards I was taken aside by one of the London staff. He told me, firmly but in a friendly way, that I had broken one of the BBC's fundamental rules—*do not show programmes to the governors or the BCS before transmission.* The theory was that the governors should not see controversial programmes before the public because they might demand changes. Nobody had told me that—and indeed the rule had to be scrapped some years later when the governors insisted on previewing difficult programmes about Northern Ireland.

With the Governors' blessing behind us, two weeks later we ran *Lilybank* in three parts—on 14, 16 and 18 November 1977, with the titles *The fourth world, So who the hell can you go to? and The people meet the planners.* (The 'planners' were men from Glasgow District Council's Housing Department and the Scottish Development Authority, who wanted to take part). And after that November showing we were further encouraged by friendly comments from the Scottish newspapers.

But that was not the end of the matter. Alasdair Milne still did not like the *Lilybank* programme, and it was not included on any network schedule. Milne himself, however, decided to come to the Broadcasting Council's February meeting. He spoke at length about the limitations on programmes brought about by the government's low financing and about the high costs of drama, light entertainment, and other network programmes. He said that he wanted to maintain as many Scottish contributions to network as possible, but he believed that our documentaries should be used for Scottish-only output.

That inevitably led to *Lilybank*. But first our Scottish Nationalist supporter, Mrs Davidson, said that the English part of the UK simply did not understand what was happening in Scotland and that must be put right. Then our chairman, Professor Thompson, who usually maintained a low profile, spoke of the 'frightening ignorance' in England about the devolution debate. There was a 'triviality' in BBC and other news about Scotland. Next, Mr Macintosh went straight for

Lilybank. He could not understand why it had not been shown on network. If Current Affairs were to come from London only, then even with the best of intentions it would get Scotland wrong. Others followed on. Mrs Carmichael said that the argument from London was constantly shifting—sometimes complaining of the quality of the programmes, sometimes a question of staff, sometimes the system by which programmes from Scotland were accepted, and so on.

Finally, I was asked to speak. I said that we welcomed much that came from London, but that Current Affairs ought to be two-way. Every single one of our 'offers' to network for 1978–9 had been turned down. This was not acceptable. We must find some access for contributions from Scotland.

Professor Thompson added that we ought to remember the good work being done by our specialists on energy, oil and politics.

Milne said little more. But *Lilybank* appeared on the BBC schedule next month, and the one-hour version went out on BBC2 in the first week of March. That was good, but I felt that Milne never forgave me for it.

Chapter 6

The nation and its future

Lilybank was one of many productions by the Matt Spicer-David Martin collaboration. In Matt we had a highly intelligent journalist with clear political judgment and good relations with his staff, and in David an all-rounder with a quick mind and an ample ability to pick up and develop new ideas. In the newsrooms, for television we had George Sinclair, another man with long experience and good judgment, with a sharp eye and the gift of brisk phrasing. For radio the head was Charles Nairn, a quieter man, but again of sound judgment and reliability. When I arrived in Glasgow all that they needed was more support from above, more freedom and more staff.

Scottish politics at that time were lively and controversial; the challenge for us was to reflect that mood and to interpret it fully and fairly. When James Callaghan took over as Prime Minister in April 1976, he pushed hard for Scottish and Welsh Assemblies. After the failure of the first Bill early the following year, he came to an agreement with the Liberals (as noted in the 'devolution' section of Chapter 4). A fresh White Paper was published in July 1977, followed by the Second Reading on 14 November. That night Chris Baur provided a live report from Westminster, immediately after the vote. He had assembled a group of Scottish MPs, who contributed a vigorous late-night programme for us.

The Bill then went into Committee, leading to the Third Reading on 23 February 1978. Later, the Lords raised some objections, but these were overcome and the Royal Assent was given in July. In September the Prime Minister announced his intention to hold a Referendum in the spring; and in November he gave 1 March 1979 as Referendum Day.

The Act as such still had serious flaws (so some of us thought). Scotland and Wales were now treated separately, which was an improvement. But the new law looked unduly complex—in parts even more incomprehensible than usual—creating a field day for the lawyers. It also provided for some 120 members of the new Assembly, which seemed excessive and again too costly. There was a further

47

complication in an amendment achieved in committee by a London MP, though of Scottish origin—George Cunningham (then Labour). The amendment required a 'Yes' from at least 40% of all those qualified to vote. That was a figure very rarely reached by any single party elected to government in the past hundred years. In the end, 32.9% voted in favour (almost exactly the proportion of the vote that the Conservatives achieved overall in the general election four months later). The 'No' vote on the Assembly was 30.8% And 36.3% did not vote.

Politics and the Assembly were, inevitably, a major issue in BBC Scotland's news and current affairs. Soon after my arrival back in Scotland, in December 1975, Matt Spicer organised three major debates on devolution and achieved an excellent 'first' by siting the opening programme at the old Royal High School in Edinburgh, opposite the old Scottish Office and facing Arthur's Seat. It had just been converted to become the home of the Assembly, and the BBC's was the first use of the debating chamber. On 27 December 1975 a non-political debate was held, mostly with business people, followed soon afterwards by two more, this time politicals—*Do we need an Assembly?* and *Is it the kind of Assembly we want?* These were held in courtroom style, with advocates on each side and witnesses being called. The same technique was used again three years later, with Labour's John Smith 'the most polished advocate on show', shortly before the Referendum.

These two debates were followed, early in 1976, by two major documentaries. Together they were called A Country of Nations: one each about Scotland and Wales. They were political, examining the differences between Scotland and Wales, and highlighting, among many aspects, the individual approaches of Plaid Cymru and the Scott-ish Nationalists. These programmes were designed for a wide audience, as much for viewers in England as for Wales and Scotland. James Cox was the reporter, and the theme of contrasting circumstances was well developed. Later that year in *Public Account* we produced a similar programme from Germany, studying the federal system there, and in 1977 we did the same in Canada, with special attention to the political unrest in Quebec. That autumn we also explored the 'unrepresented nation' of Catalonia—as it had seemed, until its liberation after Fran-co's death.

Then there was, in 1977, the five part *Scotland 1980*. It looked in turn at oil, general economic policies and taxation, industry, defence and finally the wider expectations for Scotland. It was produced by David Martin, with James Cox and Donald MacCormick at hand. (Cox and MacCormick were part of the *Public Account* team.) The oil programme was probably the most controversial, discussing what should be done about this great new source of wealth. How should it be handled? What would Scotland receive from the settlements? How would a (possibly) separate Scotland behave in 1980? What were our options? It was a difficult series to make, and it was much helped by complaints made separately by two Conservative MPs and one Labour MP. They made their objections public, bringing us a shoal of letters. Good!

Later in 1977, again under Matt Spicer's management, came *Who are the SNP?* This was an impartial examination of the Nationalists as a party and of some individual MPs—where they came from, their background, their capabilities and so on. Among others, it brought to the fore Douglas Henderson, who had recently returned from many years as an engineer in South Africa. Another was Ian MacCormick, son of one of the founders of the SNP (John MacDonald MacCormick) and brother of Professor Donald Neil MacCormick of Edinburgh University (a distinguished lawyer, himself an SNP candidate in the later 1979 campaign). Their cousin was the BBC's Donald MacCormick, who was just about to move from Queen Margaret Drive to London.

In the early spring of 1977 came Michael Buerk's first six-part series for us, *The Energy File*. This study, which was the first to be requested directly from London, focussed on oil. With Buerk was a frequent reporter Andrew Neil, now better known as the editor of *The Sunday Times*. They began with the discovery and exploration of off-shore oil; then the ownership and methods of the oil companies, and how they were financially constructed. Next came an analysis of how communities in Scotland—especially Aberdeen and Peterhead—were coping with the strains and pressures. The fourth was on the methods of sub-sea work, the fifth about the dangers and safety measures. The final programme explored alternative power sources—wind, wave and others. It was a highly relevant series for that time and for the future.

That series involved a visit to the United States, and as a result the fifth of the six programmes forecast that there would be a blow-out at one of the off-shore oil platforms. When it was broadcast there were angry complaints from offshore companies directly to the BBC's Governors. But ten days later there was just such a blow-out at the Ekofisk platform—the first to catch fire in the North Sea.

Later, as a sequel and to pull together earlier Scottish programmes for UK network, Chris Baur wrote and presented *Does Scotland Mean It?* It covered much ground in fifty minutes and helped, we believed, to make Scottish views clearer and better understood in England. It led on to *The Power of Scotland*, already mentioned in Chapter One

(To the Front), with which Chris won the Royal Television Society's Journalism Award of 1978.

On a completely different topic, Matt Spicer set up a study of the sale of council houses—not perhaps the most exciting subject, at first sight, but of great importance to many people, both in Scotland and England. Soon after our Glasgow study, *Panorama* took it up from the English point of view and devoted an entire programme to it.

Apart from *Lilybank* at the end of 1977, there was one other series that gave me much personal satisfaction. For once it was my own idea, but it was put into action by the *Public Account* team. Since we had had a fairly continuous flow of letters and complaints from MPs, often because they did not understand the time factors, the costs and the other economic requirements of production, why not invite some Scottish Members to make their own programmes? So it was arranged. We talked to each of the parties and, with surprising speed, we got agreement.

Excluding Ministers, we held a ballot on air within each of the four parties. In proportion to the number of Scottish seats held, Labour was to have five programmes, the Conservatives three, the SNP two and one Liberal. The series was given the title *Private Members' Bills*, and each successful MP could make one programme on any topic of his own choice. We preferred something relating to their constituencies, but they all chose that anyway. Each could have two days of filming with a BBC crew (three days if there was exceptionally bad weather). They could take advice from Tom Ross, one of our senior directors, and they could use James Cox for links. These were their topics:

Dr Jeremy Bray	(Lab)	The Steel Industry
Norman Buchan	(Lab)	Industrial Democracy
Douglas Crawford	(SNP)	Roads in Perthshire
Robin Cook	(Lab)	Problem areas where Building Societies refused to give loans
Harry Ewing	(Lab)	Community Service Orders
Hamish Gray	(Con)	Facilities for the mentally handicapped
Russell Johnston	(Lib)	Transport in the Highlands
Dr Maurice Miller	(Lab)	The plight of the deaf
Sir Hector Monro	(Con)	Problems over the A74/A75 roads
Iain Sproat	(Con)	Telephones for OAPs
George Thompson	(SNP)	Forestry in Galloway

By far the best, in my view, was Russell Johnston. He talked us into providing a helicopter for one day, because of the distances involved, and that produced some beautiful shots of him with his wife and children driving at speed along the coast of Skye. But he was also the most vigorous and effective in presenting his case, with Sir Hector Monro and Norman Buchan (mostly shot at Greenock) close behind.

There were many other interesting and valuable programmes from our Current Affairs stable. Much as I should like to list them all—and the names of those involved—it is probably better not to overload readers. There are, however, five others that must have a mention. They are primarily the work of David Martin, though with others working closely with him and Matt Spicer or myself occasionally in the offing.

First, an entirely non-political production—*Yes, but what do you do all winter?* It was a portrait of a village in Strathdon, in north Aberdeenshire, in each of four seasons. There was no dialogue as such—only the sounds of the air and countryside, with music, poetry and some prose. It was the forerunner of a series, taking in Burns's Country, Skye, Loch Lomond and others. 'Let the area speak for itself' was the theme.

Another, of great attraction, was *Mr Menuhin's Welcome to Blair Castle*, produced by Martin and directed by James Hunter (later Head of Television in BBC Scotland). Yehudi Menuhin had said that when listening to Scottish fiddling in Perth he felt a sense of exhilaration, 'like a kennel dog given a chance to run free'. So he was invited to run free amid Scottish fiddles at Blair Castle. He was taken to Deeside and Speyside to meet famous fiddlers, and then taken to a ball at Blair, set up by BBC Scotland and the Royal Scottish Dance Society. He listened and played, including Niel Gow's Lament on the death of his second wife. It all made a brilliant sixty minutes of broadcasting and was shown five times, at least in Scotland.

Very different was *The Craftsman Therein*, an extremely difficult programme about plastic surgery. It was based on the work of highly skilled doctors and surgeons at Canniesburn Hospital in north Glasgow, in rebuilding the structure of a human face. The filming involved the cameraman, Garry Morrison, being in the operating theatre for six to eight hours. The case he recorded was of a badly injured girl from Lanarkshire. The surgeon was Dr Ian Jackson (who later became noted for the case that came to be known as 'The Boy David'— that of an abandoned child from South America, the centre of whose face had been eaten away by disease.) The producer and director was Alan Brown, on whom it placed a heavy responsibility—so much so that afterwards he was ill for some time.

The text was written and narrated by Magnus Magnussen. We

were worried about possible reactions among people watching the programme, so we invited the press in to see it the day before transmission. That worked well. It brought us a good audience, few complaints and a great deal of approval.

Yet another achievement, of a different kind: *Scottish Connection*. It explored the links, cultural and military, between Scotland and Northern Ireland: and it disclosed, at some risk, the illegal movement of arms from Scotland to Northern Ireland. (It started life as a *Current Account* investigation, until our discoveries gave it a separate status.) It showed two UDA men in Belfast meeting a man from near Glasgow, and later the sending of dynamite and home-made weapons to some supporters of the Orange Movement in Ulster. The two reporters were Jeremy Paxman (now of *Newsnight*) and our own Brian Barr. There were lengthy sessions with our lawyers, but they were eventually satisfied that the facts were correct. The programme went ahead. After the broadcast the police in Glasgow and Lanarkshire investigated further, and the man observed by our people was charged under terrorism law. He was tried at the Glasgow High Court and went to prison for two years.

Finally, in this summary, *Checkpoint*. This was in some ways comparable to *Private Members' Bills* in that it gave six individuals the opportunity to say what they wanted. The series was taken by BBC2 for network, and it asked each of the six to talk about Scotland's future. The six, in order, were Conor Cruise O'Brien, Ian Clark, Billy Connolly, Laura Grimond, Sir Robert Grieve and Joan Bakewell: an interesting and diverse group. Each of them chose their own location and their approach.

To some who watched the series, Conor Cruise O'Brien was afterwards thought to be the least effective—but that, in my view, was because what he said was complex. He had been invited because of his experience of the smaller nations and because of his originality and insight. Dr O'Brien had been a member of the Irish Foreign Service and served as a senior member of the Irish delegation to the U.N. He was the United Nations' representative in Katanga during the conflict within the Congo in 1961. He became a Dail Government Minister and was later a member of the Irish Senate. Now he had become Editor-in-Chief of *The Observer*, in London. He had the right credentials to speak about Scotland's future, but he was complex. Historically, he said, the Scots were not a nation. They were two nations, Highlanders and Lowlanders, with distinct languages and culture. The Scottish Nationalists were 'one of a current *rash* of nationalist movements', such as the Bretons in France or those in Quebec in Canada. Scottish nationalism was a healthy reaction against remote or over-centralised government 'but culturally it's a bit thin'. His message, overall, was to be wary of 'small splinter nations'.

Ian Clark followed, with an account of how the coming of offshore oil had affected Shetland, where he was chief executive to the Island Council. It was currently creating new roads, new harbours, new houses (for the incomers and for Shetlanders), bringing more jobs and more money—but he warned that great care would be needed to maintain the distinct character of the Shetland Islands.

The comedian Billy Connolly was brisk and very entertaining, as expected, but with a message. His closing words, delivered in the football stadium at Hampden Park, included this ironic ditty remembered from his school days—

> *I am a Scottish MP*
> *From a city dreary and black*
> *And I'll shut my mouth*
> *While I'm in this House*
> *In case they send me back*

Billy Connolly did not believe that independence would work. Scotland, he said, could not stand alone. It was not viable.

Next was Laura Grimond, for many years an Orkney Council member. She spoke warmly of the island's history and unique character, and about its cattle, fishing and growing tourist trade. She spoke also of the people of Orkney having 'never been more conscious of their own heritage or more determined to fight for their own future'. It was particularly memorable because she delivered it perched on a rock high above the sea and apparently without support, at Yesnaby on the Atlantic coast—a stunning location.

The fifth was Sir Robert Grieve's, to my mind the most successful of the series. He was (and still is) a man of great character, with a deep feeling both for the Highlands and for Scotland's cities. He had long experience in the civil service and as a university academic. He had been the first Chairman of the Highlands and Islands Development Board. Sir Robert spoke of a 'cry from the mountains' and of the 'hard lands of Glasgow'. He compared Scotland with a small country like Holland 'with its many handicaps and yet managing to maximise its potential because of its self-belief. With determination, a country such as Scotland, with its much smaller population, could do as much, but the Scots had never shown the overt *self-belief* that they needed. The people of Scotland were not aware of their ability. 'I'm feart', he said. We Scots had to pull ourselves together.

The producer of Grieve's film was Patrick Chalmers, at that time head of the Aberdeen unit—of which more comes in the next chapter—and later, from 1983 to 1991, BBC Scotland's Controller. He recalls an event when Grieve's programme was broadcast. Chalmers was on holiday in a remote part of France, and he heard of the row only when he got back. He had given Bob Grieve 'a fair amount of rope', and at the close of the programme Pat Chalmers used a shot of Grieve on the esplanade of Edinburgh Castle. There Grieve spoke of his feeling for Scotland and of how it was the mainspring of his life. He ended with a story of the Edinburgh Tattoo—probably the first ever—closing with the lone piper on the battlements above. The piper played the *Last Post* and *The Flowers of the Forest*. As the sound died away there had come an emotional cry from a somewhat inebriated Glaswegian in the crowd: 'It's the greatest fuckin' country in the world!'

That had been used by Pat over the end credits, and although he knew nothing of it until returning from his holiday, there had been 'the mother and father of a row'. As a result Alasdair Milne, Managing Director of Television, had ruled that all 'fucks' must be referred to him. But as Chalmers said, it was the kind of thing that many Scotsmen would say in such a case.

Back to more serious matters. To end the series we had Joan Bakewell, to discuss the possible effects of nationalism on the arts: on our music and poetry, our painting and sculpture. It was a worthwhile contribution, suggesting that the culture of Scotland was quite capable of flourishing on its own.

Before we move on to religion, sport and later the coming development of a true Radio Scotland, it is right to name others in the News and Current Affairs groups. Some have already been mentioned: George Sinclair, as Head of Television News, Matt Spicer as Senior Producer in tv current affairs; David Martin, in charge of documentaries; Charles Nairn in charge of Good Morning Scotland, Geoffrey Cameron heading radio current affairs and Tom Ross, one of the hardest worked and most valued. Similarly the always reliable James Cox was another in constant demand. He is now frequently seen on *Newsnight* in London, when not abroad.

Among younger people were Kenneth Cargill, then a producer and, since 1988, BBC Scotland's Head of News, Current Affairs and Sport; John Milne, one of those with a steady mind and of reliable judgment (now, amongst other things, presenter of BBC Scotland's lunchtime radio news). Bill Hamilton, who did much to improve our reporting from Aberdeen in 1976–7, afterwards in Glasgow—another now seen world-wide; Brian Barr, a fast mover who made some notable programmes, stirring up much dust on the way; and Kenneth Roy, doubling with much skill between news and religious affairs—and anyone who could present *Reporting Scotland* for eight years deserves a medal.

I list these because they come quickly to mind. There were many others worthy of note. But, you may ask, no women? No, most regrettably none among the higher levels in my time—not in news and current affairs, that is. I would have liked to see that put right, for at *The Guardian* women had done very well, both at home and abroad. We had Mary Marquis, of course, frequently presenting the tv news, and Joanna Hickson similarly for radio. Kirsty Wark, too, had just joined us, and was already showing the promise that was to come. But the BBC—not only in Scotland—was slow to promote women. It is doing a little better these days.

David Barlow deserves a section of his own. He was the first real Chief Assistant that I had. At the beginning of my time there had been a man who was supposed to work with me, along with other duties, but early on he was forced to leave because of illness. Since I had never had anyone of the kind at *The Guardian* I felt no need for a replacement and there was a gap, during which someone from London came to write the minutes of the Broadcasting Council once a month.

In the autumn of 1977, however, I was asked if I would accept David Barlow as Chief Assistant. He knew his way through both radio and television, having worked in both, and he was willing to come to Glasgow for six months. Whose idea it was I do not remember—most probably Ian Trethowan's himself, for the suggestion came soon after his first visit to Scotland as DG.

David turned out to be a godsend. I could talk freely to him in a way that was possible to few of the staff. Brendon Slamin, the engineer, was the one with whom I could most readily exchange thoughts, though there were others who gave good advice. David Barlow settled in quickly, discovering what was going well in BBC Scotland and what was amiss, and he kept me in touch with much that I might have missed otherwise. He had an easy way of talking to people of many levels within the BBC, and was friendly and considerate to all. Most valuable to me, David never hesitated to tell me if he thought I was making a wrong move. He also liked walking, which meant that we could go out for an hour or a day, combining talk about work with talk that had nothing to do with the BBC. He left in April of 1978, having done his six months with us, but he continued to find reasons to visit Scotland from time to time—and indeed, 14 years later, still does.

David went on to be the BBC's Secretary, a difficult job, and more recently he has held the post of Controller Information and International Relations. Long may he prosper.

Chapter 7

Church and Nation

John Reith was a strict man of the Church whose standards dominated the BBC in its early years and long after he had left. We owe a great deal to him. In his time television was never seen as likely to overtake radio, nor was it seen that American television's acceptance of violence and brutality would find its way into part of British broadcasting. Even in the sixties and early seventies, the Church of Scotland could see itself as a powerful force in Scottish life, with the Catholics strong in Strathclyde. Already, though, attendance was dwindling in the Church of Scotland—and, in essence, what follows in this chapter is about the endeavour of BBC Scotland's religious staff to meet a changing world.

To face this was the first task of our Head of Religion, the Rev Ian Mackenzie. He was an original and deep thinking man. He had been with the BBC in Glasgow for about two years when I arrived; earlier he had been Assistant Minister at St Giles in Edinburgh and later Executive Producer of Religious Programmes with ABC Television in London and then with LWT. After that, from 1969 to 73, he had been Minister at the Old Parish Church at Peterhead before coming to the BBC. When going to Peterhead he had expected to stay there for most of his life, and he was happy with his work there. But when the BBC post became vacant he was an obvious choice, and he was urged on by other more senior ministers who thought highly of his work.

For Mackenzie, though, there was an immediate problem. For many years, until shortly before his appointment, the BBC's religious staff in Scotland had concentrated on Sunday morning church services, broadcast live, together with later recordings of two *Songs of Praise* and then a Monday programme for schools. It was an exhausting job for the staff and the morning worship was reaching only a small audience. Mackenzie, from the start, believed that he must try to reach a wider audience and had said so when interviewed. That had been accepted, and later the acting Controller, Patrick Walker, had encouraged him to proceed. He and others of the senior staff believed that the radio side was going reasonably well, but that television must make better use of film and of studio programmes. They agreed that a wider audience must be sought—non-Church people among them—and that the BBC staff must have time to think and plan new programmes. Inevitably it meant a sharp reduction of 'Worship' programmes.

That, however, went down very badly with the Church of Scotland. A cry grew up: why the loss of church services? Was the BBC abandoning them? The Church was already aware that it faced a reduction in numbers and influence. They now felt betrayed by the BBC and by Ian Mackenzie. There were a number of letters to Queen Margaret Drive, and there was another factor of which Mackenzie did not know in any detail at the time. A campaign against BBC Scotland's religious policy came to life, encouraged sad to say by the man who for many years, until 1972, had been the BBC'S Head of Religion. He was Ronald Falconer, a man of justifiably high reputation, and in the past a friend and supporter of Mackenzie. It was not helpful that, from his position as Convenor of the Church of Scotland's publicity committee, he orchestrated opposition to Mackenzie's strategy. When someone of Falconer's standing said of Mackenzie 'This man is ruining it all', why should Church Ministers disbelieve him?

Ian Mackenzie, however, had a straight response. 'The only thing— deliver the goods.' He was not going to back-track. The critics, given time, would see the sense of his efforts to reach a much wider audience (as later most of them did). As things were, the number watching a Sunday morning service was normally so small that the programme would not register in BBC records.

Looking back, he says this—'To my mind the function of television worship was best served by the *Songs of Praise* slot, for two reasons. It reached a significant audience—and still does—and it has been the great, incredible, survivor of religious broadcasting, because it just happens to touch a nerve in our folk culture: no matter how atheist or secular or humanist or semi-detached people get from religion, they still respond to hymns because hymns are deeply embedded in the folk consciousness, both privately and publicly. And the *Songs of Praise* format, which was improved about that time—it became more documentary, with filmed interviews—was perfectly designed for that. That is mainly why it has survived.

'It caught the essence in hymn singing—normally in a church— and it created that huge audience, of whom I'd guess that half never went to church from year to year. That seemed to me to be keeping the integrity of the content while being missionary in its effect.'

From experience, Mackenzie believed that the straight televising of 'Worship' could turn people away from religion. It could be dire: a man in black on a pulpit, talking for 15 or 20 minutes, or with people looking at an undistinguished stained-glass window or vases of flowers.

The Sunday evening *Songs of Praise* broke through these visual cliches by direct human contact.

At this point I come in. Within two or three weeks of my arrival at Queen Margaret Drive, at the beginning of December 1975, a letter came asking me to meet the Church and Nation Committee. I readily agreed, and 23 February was set as the date (as noted in Chapter 1). That meeting was abruptly stopped on the day by a message from the Director General, Charles Curran, demanding my immediate return to Glasgow—most embarrassing to me and annoying to the Church Committee. They kindly agreed to resume the discussion a month later, and we did make progress in understanding each others' views. By then, I believe, they were beginning to see the value of Mackenzie's initiative. In that we had good help from the Rev James Ross, Minister of Paisley Abbey and a member of our Broadcasting Council.

At that time I also took the precaution of visiting both Cardinal Gray in Edinburgh and Archbishop Winning in Glasgow. Each received me kindly, though from Winning there was a firm reminder (quite justified) that Catholics received much less attention from the BBC in Scotland than was given to the Church of Scotland. That had happened primarily because of the Presbyterian stance of Ronald Falconer in his long term of management.

Meanwhile our cut-back on Sunday morning church services still left a Scottish service every two months, but for economy these had to fit in with *Songs of Praise*, which were costly, but normally covered by UK network money. At the same time Mackenzie wanted to develop new programmes—above all, various Scottish series with a Scottish flavour and a more popular style of presentation. One such which quickly became most popular was *We've Got a Hymn*. It was produced at High Carntyne Church, in the east end of Glasgow, in a new housing area. It was not a distinguished building, but the Minister, Jim Martin, had a breezy and friendly style. His church was full, because of his way with people; and with him for the programmes was Fiona Kennedy, a very attractive and sincere singer with a melting style. People sent in their requests for hymns. The audience figures shot up—sometimes to almost twice the level of *Songs of Praise*.

That upset the people in London, who became 'twitchy' over their loss of viewers. Later Scotland pioneered by appointing a music adviser—and London's *Songs of Praise* followed that too. The Scottish adviser, Jim Clark, from Ayrshire, was very good at getting congregations and choirs to make a clear and emotional sound, in their own natural and local style.

Another change of policy was to experiment with studio programmes on Sunday mornings—for example with sermons, 20 minutes long, with the speaker addressing the tv audience at home. That was thought to work well, so it was followed by an evening parallel—*The Spirit of Scotland*. Going out at evening peak time, it invited individuals to lecture for 40 minutes. That too went well. Among the contributors were the poet George Bruce, the Very Rev Professor Robin Barbour, followed by Bishop Michael Hare Duke, Elizabeth Whitley on the traditions of the Covenanters, the musician John Currie, lawyers, historians and academics. Each was asked to relate his or her subject to the Scottish situation as it was at the time, with the Referendum and the Assembly not far off.

After each of those lectures, listeners were invited to write or visit our offices if they wanted transcripts. The result was an average of about one thousand requests for each lecture. Memorable to Ian Mackenzie was the experience, one Monday morning, of encountering a man who had hitched from Cumbernauld—clearly an unemployed man of working class, aged about 40. He had come specially to ask for a transcript. Those *Spirit of Scotland* programmes were, among other things, a reply to those who said that BBC Scotland had abandoned serious religion.

A further successful experiment was to employ a highly skilled cameraman turned director, who had moved up from London to adopt a religious lifestyle in Perthshire. Mackenzie wanted to try him out as a possible recruit, but for two years he refused, on religious grounds. He finally agreed to one project, and Mackenzie sent him off to Inverness, as a test, to produce a 20 minute film. Inverness was chosen as being a junction between the old life of agriculture, fishing and tourism (and within the Gaelic region) and the new life of oil and industry. Almost the whole film was shot on Inverness railway station, with 100 shots on the first day alone. By meeting people coming off or getting on to trains, Paul Streather made what Mackenzie speaks of as a 'brilliant' film. He had simply got the travellers to talk about values, with freedom to say what they wanted. It was not 'clouded by theologising'.

Paul Streather went on, building on *Eighth Day* to the *Yes, No, Don't Know Show*—in both, for the first time, with Kenneth Roy. These two together were very effective, with Roy, hitherto a news man, proving to have a pleasant way of moving up and down a studio audience, encouraging people to speak their minds as they wished, but not for too long. (It was long before *The Time, The Place* and *Kilroy*, which now use much the same methods.) *Eighth Day* discussed Christian ethics and the implications for society—a difficult topic at any time, and run live on a Sunday night. *Yes, No, Don't Know*, also in studio on a Sunday evening, debated matters such as 'Was Jesus God?'. Others of that kind followed. These programmes, however, were shock-horror to some of BBC Scotland's Religious Advisory Committee. They objected first that some people taking part were not Christians and had said blasphemous things, second that the Christian religion was not always winning the votes in the debates, and third that it was chaotic, not intellectually sound. At the same time the audience figures were 'rocketing'. At my meeting with the Church and Nation Committee, this time accompanied by Ian Mackenzie, when asked about these programmes I reminded them of the much higher audience figures. Did they think it all bad? There was, I think, not much response.

Ian Mackenzie was doing his utmost to bring a new and wider understanding of a changing world—changes that some of the more senior Church of Scotland people did not always recognise. He felt it his duty to promote debate and discussion, while at the same time Mackenzie himself was fully committed to his Church. He was intent, among many other things, on seeing that the film crew knew what he was trying to achieve and they loved working for him in return. He was, and is, a most unusual individual, introspective and of constantly questing intellect, a man whom I always respected.

His last major production in my time was *Coast to Coast*—as he put it, a film of metaphor, debate, issues in communities, and, not to be forgotten, worship. The first series had eight programmes, and other series followed. For each of the eight he took both the Sunday 6.40 and 10pm slots. Each programme linked two, three or four areas of Scotland, joining them up as if talking to each other (all recorded beforehand, of course). Thus he could begin with two verses of song from Dornoch Cathedral, with two following verses from the Gaelic speakers in their tiny church in Tongue, continue with singing from the Borders and finally from Fife. It was edited to bring a perfect merging. They were, in effect, singing to each other. With the same grouping, in the 10pm slot, they were linked again with interviews, talk, and the full use of the talents of the top Glasgow camera-men.

Later, with video equipment now available for outdoor production, Mackenzie produced a beautiful film with Orkney children in different islands, followed by a debate outside St Magnus Cathedral in Kirkwall, on the topic of the threat of nuclear waste. He went on to George Mackay Brown meditating inside the Cathedral, ending the pro-gramme with *Songs of Praise* from Orkney. After that he moved on to Caithness and Dounreay.

Then, as now, Scotland faced serious issues. Mackenzie believed that as the institutional church declined, broadcasting had a key role in promoting spiritual understanding; and that an endemic seriousness in the average Scot's perception of religion deserves a Scottish emphasis in religious broadcasting. His contribution to that understanding during his years with BBC Scotland were to the great benefit of Church and Nation.

Chapter 8

Gaelic, Farming, Music, Money and Sport

Gaelic

The Gaelic language and its people were a wonder and a worry. Only a small number of Scots now spoke the language, but many non-Gaels, including myself, felt that its survival as a living language was of great importance to the nation as a whole. We wanted to foster its use in the younger generation, but there was a dilemma: could we have bi-lingual programmes or were they an insult to Gaeldom? When I first arrived on the scene the Head of Gaelic, Fred Macaulay, accepted the mixing because it was the way to get his programmes on air. At heart, however, it was fairly clear that he and others wanted Gaelic to stand on its own. The one and only Gaelic television man—planner, producer and director all in one—was even more positive in that view. He was Neil Fraser, who later became Head of Radio for all Scotland. A third party was William Carrochar, then a freelance after years in the Foreign Office and service abroad. For some years he had presented *Ceilidh-air-Carrochar*, a popular bilingual series of talk and music going out on radio to the whole of Scotland.

In 1976 Carrochar became the first manager of Radio Highland, based in Inverness, and for a year or more he and the Gaelic staff of five or six young men and women maintained his bi-lingual programmes. But the pressure from Neil Fraser, and to an extent from Fred Macaulay, had its effect both in Queen Margaret Drive and in Inverness. There was pressure also for Gaelic-only programmes from distingished people in the Western Isles. I therefore accepted their view—but the result was an immediate drop in audience numbers. So Gaelic went from early evening to late evening, at least for a time.

Neil Fraser, meanwhile, had been running a weekly tv talk programme for six months every year. It went out from Aberdeen, to the north and west, and was not seen in Central Scotland. It was a live discussion with five people round the table—*Bonn Comhraidh*. This had to be slotted in between two UK network programmes, which often meant that the talk had to be carried on for an extra ten or 15 minutes because London was running late. The programme had originally been chaired by Farquhar Macintosh, but by 1976, in Neil Fraser's time as producer, it was chaired by Martin Macdonald, an experienced freelance journalist from Stornoway.

The Gaels wanted programmes in their own language. About half of them lived in Central Scotland and were thus deprived of Aberdeen's output. So in 1976 Neil Fraser made an all-Scotland programme—about the condition of housing in the island of Colonsay—with English sub-titles. That went well enough, but it required a lot of time, with limited equipment, to provide subtitles even for a 25 minute programme, and the experiment was not repeated.

In 1978, however, Neil produced a comedy series in Gaelic which quickly drew big audiences among those who could understand the language—so much so that at five minutes after 10pm a great wedding in Stornoway was interrupted while everyone adjourned to the TV lounge of the biggest hotel to watch Norman Maclean's programme, *Tormod Air Telly*. Six of those programmes went out to all Scotland at 10.15 pm.

In radio, meanwhile, Radio Highland was providing half an hour or more of topical programmes in Gaelic every weekday evening. But there were fierce differences over policy between Carrochar in Inverness and Macaulay in Glasgow, which had to be resolved in a friendly way, as they eventually were by Patrick Walker on my behalf. Carrochar had resented Macaulay's interference in Radio Highland's affairs. A fine old Gaelic saying was used by Pat Walker, though I do not know where he got it—from Neil, probably. Translated, it said 'The torrent has come face to face with the waterfall'. That settled it.

Farming

When I first met him, Patrick Chalmers was a brisk and busy man in his early thirties and, since 1970, Senior Producer in charge of the BBC's Aberdeen operations. He was the first BBC man to invite me to stay a night at his home—a beautiful place surrounded by agricultural land, including his own small farm, to the north-west of Aberdeen. The main bathroom in the house had a list of instructions to the three small daughters on what they must do first thing in the morning, so I took care to clean my teeth, tidy my hair and make sure I had the right clothes on before going down to breakfast. A charming family, not in the least overawed by their father's formidable reputation.

Pat himself had been at the North of Scotland Agricultural College before going on to Durham University. He joined the BBC in Edinburgh in 1963 and had been moved back to Aberdeen by Alasdair Milne in 1970. Later—my last appointment, in December 1978—he became

BBC Scotland's first Head of Television, based in Glasgow; and in 1983, after a period in London, he became Controller of BBC Scotland. In December 1991 he left to take up the first such post as Director of BBC's World Service Television, based in Hong Kong, also covering Japan and Australasia. He left Scotland having had the second longest run as Controller, BBC Scotland.

In Aberdeen Chalmers spent most of his time looking after the farming and other agricultural programmes. The routine work of the station was left to a very efficient administrator with long experience and knowledge of Aberdeen. Pat preferred to get out and about to organise programmes. Not long after I had taken up my job in Scotland, the Head of Administration in Glasgow suggested to me that Chalmers should be summoned to see me, to be hauled over the coals. *Why?* I asked. *Because whenever the Head of Admin rang Aberdeen, Chalmers was never in the office*—so I was told. *So what?* was my reply. He was producing excellent tv programmes on farming and related matters at amazingly low costs and the more he went out to do that the better for us. There was no cause for criticism.

Chalmers had in fact done a deal with the BBC in Birmingham and with RTE in Ireland, by which the three producers divided the work and the money. The series was called *Farm Forum* (but was later changed to *Landward*). (Also based in Aberdeen, radio was running a daily lunchtime *Farm Journal*.) According to Pat Chalmers they were 'left free to do what they wanted, like journalists writing a column'. People seemed to enjoy watching them, even when they had no direct concern with farming or other land affairs. The Aberdeen outfit had its own camera crew and from time to time they went abroad to France, Italy and elsewhere, again at very low cost. They won 'The Silver Ear' three times in the Berlin competitions. Their prizes stand in the Aberdeen office today.

Later—in my time, as it happened, but entirely the work of Chalmers and his crew—they extended their programmes into wider interests, with *Breathing Space*. It explored a number of interests in the countryside - which at that time was not as common a topic as today (in newspapers and magazines as much as in radio and television). The principal presenters were Derek Cooper and Jan Leeming, and it turned into a very successful series—each programme a 'mini-documentary', according to Pat. Among those working on the series was a bright young man newly out of Cambridge University—Keith Alexander, later Head of Arts in Glasgow and now highly placed with the BBC in London. In Aberdeen *The Food Programme* followed, with much the same people.

Later still there came an Aberdeen internal creation, The *Beechgrove*

Garden, named after the trees that grew round the BBC buildings. It was directed at first by Michael Marshall, who later left to set up his own film company in Ellon, north of Aberdeen. *The Garden* has gone on for many years, with continuing popularity.

On radio, too, there was expansion from late 1978 onwards. Until the transmitter changes world wide that winter (more fully explained in Chapters 2 and 9) radio broadcasts from Aberdeen were severely restricted. They were only possible either as part of Scotland's 'opt-out', taking over the Radio 4 transmitters for up to five or six hours a day north of Newcastle and Carlisle, or by broadcasting only to a small area round Aberdeen. Whatever was done inevitably angered many people who wanted to hear London's Radio 4. It also annoyed people in the Western Isles, Inverness, Caithness and Sutherland, Orkney and Shetland, who were not concerned with Grampian affairs. Since the winter of 1978–9 Aberdeen has been able to carry more news and programmes from its own area and to contribute both to Radio Scotland and to England. Planning the changes proved a struggle, but it worked.

Two Orchestras or One?

BBC Scotland enjoyed two orchestras, differing in structure and style. The Scottish Symphony Orchestra played classical music, the Scottish Radio Orchestra mainly popular light music. The musicians were badly paid, and it was well known that many of them were supplementing their income by 'moonlighting'—teaching, or working elsewhere. To me that seemed an unsatisfactory way of life, but apart from warranted dissatisfaction with their salaries most of them seemed to enjoy their double lives.

The Symphony Orchestra was the larger of the two—and no doubt the finer in the opinion of our Radio 3 and 4 listeners—but in 1976 and 1977 the Radio Orchestra contributed to UK network almost twice as much as the Symphony Orchestra, most of their output going to Radio 2. In 1977, however, a change of policy in Radio 2 meant that our popular orchestra was now to be used less frequently. The immediate proposal from London was that we should simply scrap the Radio Orchestra, but with the advice and encouragement of our Head of Music—Martin Dalby, an Aberdonian who had studied at the Royal College of Music and for a further two years in Italy—we fought hard to retain it.

As a precaution, however, Dalby produced an alternative scheme by which there would be an amalgamation of the two orchestras, reducing the permanent staff numbers, but bringing in extra players for major events requiring a large orchestra, such as performances of the big works of Mahler, or Stravinsky's *Rite of Spring*. At the time it seemed too drastic a step and we successfully fought the battle to retain both orchestras. Had we amalgamated them at that time, however, we might have prevented the greater loss soon after I left Queen Margaret Drive, when the Radio Orchestra was finally disbanded and even the existence of the SSO itself was threatened. It is some consolation that Dalby says that almost all of those who lost their jobs did well eventually, though not all in the field of music—one, for example, is now 'Head of Brass' at Eton, another deals in antiques, and a third runs a pub in Spain. Dalby himself has now been in his post for twenty years.

In my time, mainly thanks to Dalby and others, the Symphony Orchestra extended its public activities. It had acquired a fine reputation and in late February and early March of 1977 the whole orchestra went to Hong Kong, where they gave eight concerts and were very well received. (Visits to Europe followed somewhat later, in Patrick Chalmers's time.) At home, in the seventies, the orchestra began to give many more public performances than before. Instead of occasional concerts in Glasgow's City Hall and infrequently in Edinburgh's Usher Hall, the orchestra began to perform every second week throughout the winter and spring in Glasgow, appeared frequently in Edinburgh and Aberdeen, and gave concerts in Ayr and Oban at least once a year, building an enthusiastic and appreciative following throughout the country. Soon afterwards, too, regular performances began at Stirling University's MacRobert Centre, leading on to a regular season of ten concerts every winter. All that was good, but there were two misfires. One was the use of a publicity company which went to the wall, taking good BBC money with it. The other was our failure to persuade John Pickles (who dominates Chapter 9) to take live music from our orchestras for the new Radio Scotland, because he was thinking in Radio 2 terms—a battle fought by Dalby for weeks before the station opened, of which I was unaware until too late.

A very successful initiative at the end of 1977 was to start making commercial recordings by the Symphony Orchestra. At the beginning they concentrated on recording Scottish songs with a full orchestra and choir, producing a magnificently stirring sound. Later they were able to progress to a much wider range. Under several distinguished conductors the SSO have produced an orchestral sound which is almost immediately identifable as their own. Considering that early in my time back in Scotland there had been thoughts of closing down all BBC's Scottish music makers, we—they—weathered a difficult and worrying time remarkably well.

Money

Bryan Mitchell was our man—the first Head of Finance outside London, and the first for any region. It was, he says, a form of financial devolution. Until April of 1977 Mitchell was in the contracts department, but seven months earlier, in September 1976, Michael Checkland (Controller, Planning) came to Glasgow to prepare for a new system in Scotland. Checkland had interviewed three people, taking a day to do it. He then instructed Mitchell to gather a working party to report on how BBC Scotland could manage aspects of its finance—'an autonomous department', it was called. He had to report by Christmas, which he did. And that report was accepted in London. In February the post of Head of Finance was advertised. Bryan Mitchell's was the only application, and on 1 April 1977 he took up his new post.

Checkland told him not to build up an empire. In fact, for the first six months Bryan ran both his new job and the contracts department. He and his secretary, in practice, were the only new staff. They were not directly involved with the financing of particular programmes, such as television drama or tv news, but they were aware of the cash actually being spent. That meant an earlier warning when something was going wrong, instead of the old three or four months of waiting before hearing of it from London. Even so, Mitchell says, it was often a 'gut feeling' that alerted him to possible trouble. He was keeping a close eye on the way cash was going through the books.

One major achievement was the introduction of a highly advanced computer system, fully introduced in Queen Margaret Drive on 1 October 1978. Until then all information had to be 'hand recorded' in hand-written ledgers. The computers were agreed in January 1978, at a cost of about £35,000, and one of the early uses in the summer of 1978 was in helping the new Head of Radio, John Pickles, to plan his costings.

All the other regions followed Scotland's lead. All appointed their own heads of finance. Overall the new system worked much better, with earlier reporting and the virtues of 'autonomous management'. In the beginning Mitchell had to go to see Checkland in London every five or six weeks, but that was reduced once the system was running. At first he had had to visit various accountants and talk to Radio, Tv and Engineering in London. It all came together well. Checkland kept a sharp eye on what each was doing, but he was always very helpful.

As to the conflict with the Director of Finance over the charges to BBC Scotland for network programmes made in England (Chapter 4), Bryan Mitchell was not involved. He had no part in the way licence fee money collected in Scotland was allocated. He was, however, aware of the way in which Scotland, Wales and Northern Ireland were shown for many years to be in deficit—'the infamous Statement 6', as those in the National Regions saw it. This continued into the eighties, but was stopped four or five years ago. Mitchell agrees that the 'unanswered question' was the market price for network programmes. All else, in his view, was and is fair and accountable.

Sport

Three things stand out. First, it took an Irishman recruited from Belfast in 1974 to revolutionise BBC Scotland's sport. He was Malcolm Kellard, still to be heard, though technically retired. Second was Kellard's success in introducing viewers to a wide range of sports, from bowls to hockey, while still respecting the priority of football and rugby. Third is his distress at the unsporting attitudes of many Scots before and after the 1978 World Cup in Argentina—an evil attitude which he sees growing again in 1991–2.

Kellard was recruited eighteen months before my arrival to succeed Peter Thompson, who had been a legendary figure in sports broadcasting in Scotland for more than 20 years. In Queen Margaret Drive there was a wish to break away from the domination of football—and especially the focus on Rangers v Celtic matches. A wider scope was wanted, and Kellard had been doing that in his home country with clear success. He had won audiences, even for less popular sports such as indoor bowls. It happened also to be a time of great growth in sponsorship—not bringing any money to the BBC itself, but with coordination, so that extra money was going towards the organisers of sporting events of interest to the broadcasters, though with advertisements visible in the background. According to Kellard, companies came along for a quiet chat and were told that if they secured high profile people for a match likely to interest Scots, then, yes, the BBC would be there.

The bowlers were among the first, with indoor matches at Coatbridge. These subsequently built into a World Championship. Outdoor matches at Queens Park led to the World Championship in Aberdeen. Together with other games, Kellard built up 36 'first time' competitions in less than two years. Bowling was amongst the most popular, coming as it did just before the snooker boom. World Title boxing matches at Glasgow's Kelvin Hall brought even more publicity. Surprisingly, there were very few complaints. According to Malcolm Kellard, the main complaints were of 'too much cricket and too little golf'—as one might expect in Scotland—or of 'too much Rangers' or 'too much Celtic'. Radio sports reporting was also covering a much wider range and doing well, in spite of having to 'opt out' of Radio 4 in London.

Kellard believes that much of his success lay in his past relations with sports people and others in London. People in Scotland tended to mistrust those in London. Arriving in Glasgow, Kellard had been astonished by hostility to the metropolis which had apparently developed over many years. Over the years Kellard, had come to know many of the senior sports reporters well—Peter Alliss, Cliff Morgan, Desmond Lynam, Harry Carpenter, David Vine. Two former national Heads of Sport, Alan Hart and Bryan Cowgill, with whom Kellard had worked, went on to become Controllers of BBC1. He continued to foster these relationships and so became aware of network plans months and sometimes years ahead—and could plan his own programmes accordingly. It was 'not exactly a spy ring', he says, but it made scheduling easier: person to person was the only way.

Within this framework, Kellard wanted to give pride of place to football, which had always provided the hard core in Scotland. But he was also determined to foster rugby, giving it Saturday air time. And within his 40 or so minutes on a Saturday night he sought also to find space for other sports—whittling away a few minutes for seven or eight minutes of hockey or curling or basketball or ski-ing. And the viewers seemed to like the new mix.

Of the 1978 World Cup Football in Argentina, he speaks sadly. Since Scotland was the only one of the home countries to qualify for the finals, the entire British interest focussed on Scotland and our nation 'went berserk'. Too many Scots believed even before they left for Buenos Aires that the Scottish team would win the World Cup. There was a huge presentation of the entire squad to a near capacity crowd at Hampden Park, which became a giant going-away party displaying strong patriotic and nationalistic emotions, boding ill for what was to follow. When the players and supporters went to South America the supporters behaved themselves, but the players let the country down both on and off the field. Generally the whole experience was one that Scottish fans and administrators would prefer to forget. It is significant that the manner in which the exercise was 'sold' has not been repeated. It did no good for Scottish sport and it further soured relations between Scotland and England, allowing those south of the border to look with increased disdain on their northern neighbours. The debacle had a political effect too—so Kellard says, and I agree—since it diminished Scottish self-confidence. To some extent it even damaged relations between BBC Scotland and the rest of the BBC.

Malcolm Kellard goes further, deploring unattractive anti-English attitudes. He sees evidence of this in the behaviour of some Scots, not only in football but now also in rugby. 'People just want to see England beaten, irrespective of the quality of the play—objectivity goes out of the window and some Scots have been blinded by an unattractive and aggressive form of nationalism', he says. He looks back at an interview with the late Archbishop of Canterbury, Dr Geoffrey Fisher, a football fan and supporter of Nottingham Forest, whose favourite television programme was BBC's Match of the Day. Kellard says 'We can see football as it should be—archbishop and shipyard worker together, enjoying the same game and respecting fine play, no matter from which side it comes, whilst maintaining healthy and patriotic support for their own country.'

Kellard recalls that most of the BBC Directors General in his time were keen sports followers, not only because sport produced some of their highest viewing figures. Ian Trethowan's special interest was in horse racing, on which he was something of an expert. It was Trethowan himself who noted that one third of all output on television and radio came from sports programmes and sports outside broadcasts.

Chapter 9

A real Radio Scotland, at last

'You must get it right in the first two weeks'. James Gordon was candid in talking to a rival. 'If you don't', he said, 'it will take you two years.' He had made a great success of Radio Clyde and he knew that the new Radio Scotland was coming. We were talking in his rural home, with its fine garden looking towards Ben Lomond, and I enjoyed listening to him. But we in the BBC did not get it quite right at first: our existing audience did not like the new style.

The story begins with the Geneva Agreement of October 1975. This was the outcome of long international negotiations to make better use of the world's transmitters, so that more could go on air without stations jamming each other—or so it was hoped. It regrouped the world's transmitters, and it set 23 November of 1978 as the starting date. Among many changes, it would give us a real Radio Scotland. No longer would we be dependent on London's Radio 4. For 18 hours a day (six am to midnight, or a little longer) we were to have our own radio station. That was welcome both to BBC Scotland and to Radio 4, since it meant that listeners had a free choice all day. They could listen to the new long-wave Radio 4 with its powerful extended transmitters, or to Radio Scotland on medium or VHF (very high frequency); and at a later date, if possible, Radio 4 was also to come on medium wave and VHF in some parts of Scotland. It meant big changes all round.

Further, our new radio station was to provide extensive reporting of the Scottish Assembly, expected in the autumn of 1979. All this led to the decision that Radio Scotland should be based in Edinburgh, with a big new building as near as possible to the old Royal High School, giving members of the Assembly easy access to our studios for interviews and debates. The opportunity was also to be taken—if the performers agreed—to move the Scottish Symphony Orchestra to Edinburgh and to provide more space for radio drama.

From mid-1976 our admirable chief engineer, Brendan Slamin, became our planning man (temporarily). With him was our chief accountant, Bryan Mitchell, another hard worker of total reliability.

71

The planners from London were also of great help—and they clearly enjoyed coming to Edinburgh. By good luck they had located an open site in the city centre, at the top of Leith Street, directly below Calton Hill. It was as good a site as anyone could want, and as close to the Royal High School as we were ever likely to find. The land belonged to the district council, with whom satisfactory terms were agreed by the end of the year.

Since that had gone well, in March of 1977, after discussion with others of the senior staff, I wrote an outline of what the new station was to do. We were very conscious of the success of James Gordon's Radio Clyde, which had gathered large audiences from the day it opened. For a mainly industrial area he had created a Scottish cross between Radios 1 and 2, but he slotted in hourly news of much higher quality than most other commercial stations. In the evening, when television attracted its big audience, and at weekends, he included classical music and discussion. (Its counterpart in Edinburgh, Radio Forth, had not done nearly so well.) Our brief was not to be simply a Scottish version of Radio 4, nor must it go too far towards Radio Clyde. It must try to attract a much broader public over the whole of Scotland.

My outline, to apply from November 1978, therefore said that our new service 'must be new and not simply copying the style and manner of any existing channel'. It went on to say that the new Radio Scotland must be 'more popular' than the existing, limited service—and that it must speak with a more distinct Scottish accent. The new service must 'start with a bang' and be more relaxed and informal than Radio 4.

It is important to recognise that in March 1977 there was common agreement on the 'more friendly' approach. The senior staff in Glasgow and Edinburgh had taken part in the planning of programmes, and there was general support. The Broadcasting Council for Scotland had been given an outline and had approved, though they did not quite absorb what they were letting themselves in for. Nor did I, for that matter. But it was entirely wrong that, twenty months later, most of the complaints about the new Radio Scotland were levelled at John Pickles. He had not even joined us in Scotland when that outline was presented. He was then in Northern Ireland, though his parental home was near Stirling. He became Head of Radio only in November 1977.

We shall come back to that. With the negotiations for the new building going well by the end of 1976, the architects set to work. That took time, and the first outline produced by the BBC's principal architect was rejected by the Royal Fine Art Commission for Scotland. They stipulated a building no higher than about four storeys, in spite of the high Calton Hill behind, and they wanted a straight facade in keeping with the existing eighteenth and nineteenth century buildings in Leith Street and to the north side of the big roundabout. The Commission took a hard line because of the anger of their predecessors some twenty-five years earlier—when, as it happened, my father was their chairman. The government of that time had allowed a 'modern' design for the new Scottish Office in the St James's Centre—a monstrous building quite out of keeping with the character of Edinburgh.

That delayed action, which in the end was a benefit. Sir Michael Swann, with his close knowledge of Edinburgh's affairs, secured a revision with the Fine Art Commission that satisfied both sides. The height was restricted and for the most part the building blended with the style of the old buildings, but it permitted a variation on the southeast side, closest to Calton Hill, which would have accommodated the needs of the BBC's Scottish Symphony Orchestra. It would have been an interesting building, but it was again postponed for financial reasons within the BBC and was finally abandoned when the Assembly failed to reach its 40% vote. (The 40% requirement was a last-minute addition to the Act, brought about by a Scottish MP who represented an English constituency; and, as already noted in Chapter 6, the vote in March 1979 was 32.9% in favour and 30.8% against.) Some years later the orchestra enjoyed a beautiful restructuring of its Glasgow home; and Radio Scotland, after enduring a period in cramped and inadequate circumstances in Edinburgh, ultimately moved its headquarters back to Glasgow's West End.

With the arrival of John Pickles as Head of Radio in the late autumn of 1977, the appointment of additional staff began—though, rightly, most of the senior posts went to people already working in radio in Glasgow, Edinburgh, Aberdeen and Inverness. By autumn of 1978 trial runs were being made in readiness for the great launch. On the news and current affairs side there were few changes, although their time on air was extended. Peter Clarke—until then a freelance—was brought in as Economics Correspondent, specifically for Radio Scotland, though with some television work as well. In preparation for the 'more popular' and 'more relaxed' style that was coming, the morning and mid-day news became more chatty—and that brought the first of many complaints. But the real test came on 23 November, when the new Radio Scotland was launched.

From that day, for two or three weeks, there was a continual flow of letters to Queen Margaret Drive and Queen Street complaining about the new style. In the newspapers, too, there was a battery of complaint. I have kept only the letters to *The Scotsman* from Thursday 30 November for eight days—though I know that there were similar reactions in the *Glasgow Herald*, the *Dundee Courier* and the *Aberdeen Press and Journal*. On the first of those days *The Scotsman* gave half a page to nine letters. The first complained that the new Radio Scotland had failed to establish 'its own national identity' and that it was 'just another Radio 2, filling in the gaps when ideas run out'. The second deplored the 'pap now being served up' and asked whether this was the standard we must expect if the people of Scotland voted Yes in the referendum. The third, while writing mostly about the transmitters, said he was sad about the lack of professionalism. Others complained about lack of international news; and the last found the new programmes 'unmentionable and totally indescribable'.

Over the next two days there were only single letters in *The Scotsman*, regretting the shortening or loss of *Thought for Today* (the brief religious daily item). But on Monday 4th there were more: complaints referred to 'a fall in standards'; one declared that the new Radio Scotland was 'modelled on English local radio' (he cannot have heard much of stations such as BBC Radio Leeds, Radio Cornwall or Radio Norfolk, all working to high standards), and another simply declared 'It's rubbish!' Another letter that day called for the immediate sacking of the broadcasters, lamenting that 'The shades of Wallace, Burns, MacDiarmid and Reith—to name but a few—must surely be doing about 4000 revs'. (Funny, but unfair.) That day, though, there were also two friendly letters.

The critical barrage continued, until on the eighth day *The Scotsman* invited John Pickles to reply. He drew attention to the wide range being offered by Radio Scotland—in its first days three plays, a symphony concert, programmes on the arts, wild life, religion, current affairs and agriculture, profiles, documentaries, daily magazines, 'live' rugby and football commentaries, popular music, folk music and jazz. Radio Scotland, he said, was not designed as a substitute for Radio 4; that was still available to listeners. In addition to Edinburgh and Glasgow, Radio Scotland was bringing in Aberdeen, Inverness, Orkney and Shetland. They were providing a rich diversity of interests, and they were concerned mainly with Scotland. In spite of all the criticism, he said, Radio Scotland knew that many people were enjoying the range of programmes.

John had taken a battering and had stood his ground. It was true that a wide range was being offered, much of which survives today, though with more international material than at that time. But the 'relaxed' presentation was a mistake when dealing with news, current affairs and other serious issues. I was as much to blame as anyone. We had not 'got it right.'

Even more serious than the letters to us and to the newspapers, there was the Broadcasting Council for Scotland. They had approved the outlines many months before, but they detested the results. The

Council members were civil, however, in the way they gave their views. The style of presentation was disliked, and there were many doubts about the mixing of the spoken word with intervals of popular music. There was criticism of the way *Good Morning Scotland* was put together. There was also distaste for the custom of backing announcements with music (the common style of commercial radio). The edging of items with talk or music was unpopular with the Council.

At the same time the Council admired the way Neville Garden was getting into stride with *Good Morning Scotland*, though several members thought that it would be better to return to a double headed system. (Neville was a recent recruit, and beyond doubt became one of the most effective of all news presenters in Scotland, in addition to his music programmes.) Kenneth Roy's presentation of *Facing Scotland* was also widely approved of, as were several others of the more serious programmes. The problem was that, as a new station operating for 18 hours a day, we were trying to reach as wide an audience as we could. Radio Clyde had succeeded brilliantly within the Glasgow and nearby areas; we were trying to do as well with the much more varied communities over the whole of Scotland. But at the start only people accustomed to listening to Radio 4 were listening to us. There had been too little promotion beforehand, and press reviews had been critical.

On the day of the Broadcasting Council's meeting—Friday December 8 (1978)—our new station had been on air for no more than two weeks. As it happened, Ian Trethowan (Director General) was due to come that day. He was travelling by road from Newcastle and had been delayed on the way. When he arrived, just as the discussion on Radio Scotland was coming to an end, he said that he had listened for two hours on his way north. On the basis of that, he said, he considered that Radio Scotland was achieving what the Council had wanted. That calmed the critics, to the relief of both John Pickles and me. It was clear, however, that some changes would be necessary.

For reasons explained in the final chapter, I gave up my post as Controller at the end of the year. I then moved to Inverness. John Pickles also departed some time afterwards, because of a serious misjudgment on his part in testing the reactions of staff on duty one night. The *gaffe* was widely reported in Scotland's press. The apparent intention was to discover how speedily and well the staff would deal with the sudden announcement 'The Queen is dead'. No prior warning of such a test had been given and the affair had unfortunate repercussions, with bitter complaints from those on duty that night. John was moved to take charge of one of the local radio stations in England.

It is worth recording, however, that in the Glasgow area BBC Radio

Scotland—now with an approach closer to Radio 4's but maintaining a strongly Scottish character—eventually rose towards audience figures not far below Radio Clyde's level. In other areas it did even better. Figures have to be treated with some caution, but from details that I secured later for my book *News in the Regions* (Macmillan, 1989) both Radio Scotland and Radio Clyde were then doing exceptionally well. The details were drawn from ILR (Independent Local Radio) and BBC research. At that time, on ILR figures, within west central Scotland Radio Clyde had a weekly 'reach' of 987,000 people, while Radio Scotland reached 467,000. That was quite good, but working on a daily rather than a weekly basis, BBC research put Radio Scotland level with Radio Clyde, partly because of the steady audience for *Good Morning Scotland*. Both studies showed Radio 4 UK in Scotland reaching about half the weekly audience of Radio Scotland.

From this and other evidence, it is clear that in spite of its troubled start, Radio Scotland in the end came out very well, though it probably took most of Jimmy Gordon's forecast of two years to put things right. Success has been achieved by the strength of its main programmes on the five weekdays—*Good Morning Scotland* from 6 to 9 am, *Head On* until 10, *Speaking Out* until 11, *MacGregor's Gathering* until 12, and *Queen Street Garden* (with Neville of that Ilk) until just before 1pm. There are variations, to provide for such items as *The Shetland Gathering* and *Corridors of Power*. Three minutes of news is given every hour on the hour, and there is half an hour of news and analysis from 1pm. The afternoon provides more variety, but *Newsdrive* comes from 4.30 until six, with a 15 minute news bulletin followed by variations throughout the evening. And on the artistic side, both in the early days of Radio Scotland and today, there were John Arnott looking after talks and features (and countryside affairs) and Stewart Conn heading Radio Drama as well as winning a string of poetry awards. Those who took part in the early launch of Radio Scotland can now regard it with great respect.

Chapter 10

The bad and the good

Mountains and politics come into this last chapter. In the series *Mountain Days*, for the first time I planned one programme and directed another. When I had first joined the BBC in 1975, Huw Wheldon told me that I must make at least one radio and one television programme each year. Now, in 1977–8, this was my first real chance to do it, and I enjoyed it greatly. The politics are a different story—involving major issues, first with the Government's White Paper on Broadcasting and then in Scotland with the approach to the Assembly. From those issues and related matters, unfortunately, my time as Controller came to an end.

I had presented an outline for the *Mountain Days* series to Brian Wenham, Controller of BBC2 in 1977. He commissioned the series of eight programmes and he came to the island of Arran to watch one afternoon's filming in the early summer of 1978. He was lifted to the top of North Goatfell in a helicopter, and he stayed to give the crew a roaring dinner that night. We were not often honoured in that way.

That film, *Three Men on the Goat*, was the fifth in a series of seven, and it was probably the best. It had been planned by me, but was greatly improved by the director—a young man, Michael Radford. The 'three men' were artists from Glasgow—one painter, one musician and one sculptor. They talked as they climbed, and then each executed his own work on or near the summit of North Goatfell. The painter, Sandy Goudie, chose the scene at the top of the ridge—a beautiful work which now hangs in Queen Street, Edinburgh. The musician— flute-player and composer George McIlwham—wrote *The Arran Rhapsody* for the programme and was filmed playing a sequence with the mountain Cir Mhor beyond. The sculptor, Archie Forrest, after climbing the hardest approach to North Goatfell, used granite rock to create a structure with two hands held up—a reminder of his climb, with a hint of terror. (When he first saw the mass of granite blocks on the north side of North Goatfell he said that nothing he could do could match their artistry.) That, too, is with the BBC in Glasgow—I wanted to buy it, but they would not let me. There was also a fourth man,

Dave Bathgate, a great mountaineer whom we took along as our safety adviser. He not only did that but talked during and after the climb with lively comment. The helicopter was needed to capture the dramatic scenery and to film the artists at work. The weather was not very kind to us, but the results were good. The crew were of the best— photography by Stuart Wyld and Andrew Dunn, director Michael Radford, producer David Hanley, and film editor Polly Moseley.

Of the others, *Rum: an Island in Time* recorded a memorable visit to the 'forbidden island', so called because for over 100 years access had been prohibited and even now, in the hands of the Nature Conservancy, access was restricted. They gave us a free run of their rugged hills and empty wilderness, most beautifully filmed by Stuart Wyld and Mike Herd. The sea eagles, the wild goats, the shattered gabbra, the birds which came out of their hides only after dark, the last owner's surprisingly beautiful mausoleum—all that and the mountains, close to the Cuillin of Skye. Some critics complained that there was no story, but that was the point: Rum was there to be seen.

For that film, and for one other, I recruited a producer from the schools department, Norman McCandlish. His second programme was *A Walk Through Winter*, along rugged parts of the Pembroke coast, ending at St Ann's Head. BBC Wales had given assent to our filming in their territory. Its Controller thought I was wrong to do it in February, but while in the army in 1942 I had seen some of that country and knew how good it could look in winter there. We recruited a young Welshwoman, Stella Mair Thomas (recommended by BBC Wales), and walking with her was Charlie Rose, mountaineer, from Torridon. They talked well as they walked. After our BBC2 network showing, BBC Wales used our programme at Christmas and several times later.

Highland Pony Trail took two men and two women through Knoydart and (without the horses) they climbed Ladhar Bheinn, looking across to Skye. Then they and the horses swam the tidal narrows of Loch Hourn before riding on northwards. It was good, but it was the only one I could not attend and I was not pleased when it turned out that the producer had overspent both in time and money. He (Bill Hook) was a lively and amusing man, but I was intent on keeping within budget. That applied at all times, but there was a special reason in the case of the *Mountain Days* series. Of that, more comes towards the end of this chapter.

Two less demanding programmes were *The Old Man of Stoer* and *Buttermere Ballads*. The *Old Man* was a climb of a rock stack, about 400 feet high, on the Sutherland coast, accessible only at low tide or by boat. The two climbers were among the best in Britain—Joe Brown, with Dave Bathgate again—together with two women of much less experience. Behind the whole operation was Hamish MacInnes, a master in these matters. Stuart Wyld was directing, as a break from operating his cameras, and as producer we had David Hanley, who was taking a holiday from being the manager of film operations, which was mostly an indoor job. David was good at cheering us up, as a summer fog prevented any work for two days. The third day mercifully brought sunshine and let us do almost all the shooting in one day.

Buttermere Ballads had a different approach: two poets talking together as they walked deep in the heart of Wordsworth's land. They were Roger McGough from Liverpool and Liz Lochhead from Glasgow—both well on their way to distinction in their art. The weather was unkind to us, so after four days on the shores of Buttermere we moved to Kendal, to let Liz and Roger take part in a discussion in the Arts Centre there. Through no fault of theirs, that was the least successful of the series. It was interesting, nevertheless.

The seventh was *Arrochar—The Cobbler*. That, for the first time, I directed myself. Stuart Wyld and Andrew Dunn were on the cameras and were a blessing to me. They needed only the simplest of direction and were quick to correct my errors. So, too, was Gordon Forsyth, in charge of sound recording. A first class team. The Cobbler, a mountain just short of 3000 feet, was one I had loved since the age of seventeen—both for its beauty and because, in days before I had a car, I could get there by train from Glasgow in just over one hour. It is a mountain with three tops, offering rock and snow approaches according to weather. I had been on the Cobbler four or five times every year when I was with the *Glasgow Herald* before going to Manchester, and almost as often when back in Scotland once more.

We made the film in two parts—the first in February, to catch the snow at its best, and then in early April in the hope of sun and a touch of spring. The climbers were an old friend, Sandy Cousins, together with his fifteen year old daughter, plus two of the toughest all-year Glasgow mountaineers. The plan was that Sandy and his daughter would climb by the main route, taking the easiest way through deep but hard snow to the summit, while the two others climbed by a difficult gully. On the second day we had excellent weather, with sun and hard snow and a view for about forty miles. But we knew we had to get everything right in one shot: no chance of a second shot, because of short daylight and the tell-tale footprints that would be left in the snow.

The gully climbers got to the summit first, as we hoped, providing excellent shots of the last seven minutes of their ascent, both from a helicopter which swept round the summit and from the fixed camera further back. To crown the day we had Sir Robert Grieve and Hamish

MacInnes, together with two other great mountaineers, arriving at the summit too. They all had a conversation before moving down. That February filming was all that anyone could have wanted; but April was horrid, with wet snow still on the tops and almost continual sleet. Still, it gave a fair impression of good and bad on Scottish mountains.

There was to have been an eighth mountain. That had been planned from the beginning and agreed with BBC2 in London. It was to be the most dramatic and most costly of the series. That was one reason why I had to keep the first seven well within budget, as we did. The plan was to climb Hadrian's Imperial Porphyry mountain, seven thousand feet high and, so far as we knew, never previously climbed—not even by Hadrian, though he lived below it for some years before being sent to Britain. It was about 15 miles inland from the town of Hurghada, on the shores of the Gulf of Suez. Hadrian had built a temple there while the stones for the Colosseum were being cut and sent to Rome. By chance, in 1966, I had seen those amazing mountains from an aircraft while going up the Gulf. Hadrian's mountain looked like a rugged, double-size Sgur nan Gillean, with three huge spires. The Egyptian government, when approached in 1978, had said that their army would give us help. They liked the whole idea. But it did not come about, for reasons explained at the end of this chapter. (Three or four years later, a British Army group made the climb.)

Now from mountains to politics, and from good days to bad ones—though still with some useful achievements to come. Much was happening in Parliament, some of it of direct concern to BBC Scotland and BBC Wales. Bruce Millan had taken over from William Ross as Secretary of State for Scotland when James Callaghan became Prime Minister in April 1976, and Millan had led the Government's call for a Scottish Assembly. At the same time the Home Secretary, Merlyn Rees, remained responsible for broadcasting. So we had, in effect, two Ministers keeping an eye on us. The summer of 1978 had brought a White Paper from the Government, proposing reforms for the BBC, mainly on Annan terms. Nearly all the proposals, Annan based, were welcome, but there were two or three items that could be damaging. So I was glad when, a few days after publication of the White Paper, Bruce Millan asked me to come for a private talk with him. And, no less, I welcomed a suggestion from Merlyn Rees that he should pay a more formal visit to Queen Margaret Drive. He came four weeks later, on his way back from staying with the Queen at Balmoral.

The two main worries about the White Paper were to some extent linked. The Government wanted to alter the way the BBC's Governors appointed the top 30 or so of the staff. The White Paper called for three

Service Management Boards, with the Government itself having a part in appointments, although the BBC's Governors would still formally make the final decisions. The three, much as before, would be Boards for television, radio and external broadcasting. As to Scotland and Wales, appointments of council members were to be subject to Ministers' approval. The BBC's old system of using advisory groups for Wales and Scotland would be at an end. (That had worked well in the past, odd as it might seem.) The BBC's Governors themselves, as before, would be appointed by the Crown on the advice of the Home Secretary.

In talking to Bruce Millan (31 August 1978), I said that our Broadcasting Council—due to meet next day—would welcome many things in the Paper. One was 'local' radio (the White Paper's term), with greater output from Aberdeen, possibly another such for Tayside, and development for the Borders, Dumfries and Galloway, and the Western Isles. The smaller stations would follow the achievements of Orkney and Shetland, which were doing very well. The BCS would also welcome the retention of the licence fee as the BBC's main source of money, because it helped to secure independence. All that went well with Millan.

There were, however, two or three points less welcome to us in Scotland. As he knew—and had kindly spoken on my side—there had been a blindness in parts of the BBC in London to the needs of Scotland. We had achieved much in the past two years, but we still needed more of the promised 'autonomy'. With the new Service Management Boards, we looked like having to spend even more time talking to people in London. Autonomy was still a long way away. Bruce acknowledged this, but was more optimistic than I was.

Beyond that, what about our Broadcasting Council? If civil servants were to advise Ministers on its membership, they were likely to be cautious. We were not so worried about political interference; we feared dullness. We had a lively lot now. Would that continue? Bruce said he did not believe that there was any such danger. The system would not lead to political appointments; it would be too obvious. Within Scotland the same names kept coming up. Ministers would welcome suggestions for new names. There would be informal consultation before a list went to the Secretary of State. He thought I was being unfair to the civil service, though he recognised the need for 'fresh blood and independence of mind'.

He spoke of the Government's intention that the new Management Boards should bring delegation within the BBC. The alternative was to break up the BBC. Bruce himself was against that. He accepted that it was a great institution which had done much for broadcasting. In general it worked well, but there was something wrong with its system at the top. He knew that the proposed structure was complex, but was it any more complex than the present BBC structure? The DG would still be excessively powerful.

He asked, with a friendly smile, *to whom was I accountable?* My reply was that, apart from the BCS, the answer was much too long. (I was answerable to at least seven people in London—DG, MDTv, MD Radio, D Finance, D Public Affairs, D Personnel and D News and Current Affairs.) That was one of the troubles and one of the reasons why I had had to waste so much time travelling to and from London. But, I said, a little less than truthfully, things were getting better. Finally, he said that he had been worried before the White Paper that Wales, with half its output in Welsh, would be thought to have put on too strong a performance; but there had been very little reaction from Gaeldom.

Four weeks later Merlyn Rees arrived on his way home from Balmoral. He came at 11.45, talked to me alone for twenty minutes, and then toured the Queen Margaret Drive building. He lunched with our senior staff—16 in all—and spoke briefly to them at the end. He then went off to Radio Clyde and to Scottish TV, and in the evening, with his wife, he came to dinner in my flat not far from the BBC. Other guests were his secretary, together with Brendon Slamin (another Welshman, and one of our most constructive men) and Patrick Walker. I cooked dinner (braised beef, plums and cheesecake, stilton) having got home only about fifty minutes before the visitors came. Armed plain-clothed policemen were discreetly placed outside. (Rees had been Northern Ireland's Secretary before the Home Office.) Mrs Rees had been given a large haunch of venison by the Queen, and she wanted advice on how to cook it. I had not the remotest idea, but rang an aunt who told me how it should be done. It was a pleasant evening— I hope—with no politics in it.

Rees had made no commitments beyond the White Paper. He had agreed that different arrangements were needed for Scotland and for Wales, and he had insisted that appointments to Broadcasting Councils must be a matter for Ministers. The Referenda on devolution for Wales and Scotland were still to come (on 1 March 1979).

So far, not so bad. But in the autumn the whole outlook darkened. There were three elements: first, a press conference during which, answering a question, I said once again that we were not getting a fair deal from London in the commissioning of network programmes. That was followed by a personal 'annual report' to the Director General (a standard BBC routine), written by Alasdair Milne for television and Aubrey Singer for radio, saying that I was not fit for my post. And, third, there was the row with the Broadcasting Council itself, the first and only one I ever had with them, over the style and nature of the new Radio Scotland. Taken together, these left me feeling that my time as Controller was nearing its end.

The press conference, as such, need not have been harmful. It was held in September at the request of the BCS, to report the Council's views on the government's White Paper on Broadcasting. Professor Thompson was in the chair, but I had to do most of the talking. As agreed with the Council, I said that there was much in the Government's plans that we welcomed—the freedom of broadcasters from political or party direction, the greater 'autonomy' to be given to Scottish and Welsh Councils, and the need to counter what Annan had called the 'vicious circle' by which our talent was drained away. But I also said, as I had said before, that we in Scotland felt that although there had been a great improvement we were still not getting a fair deal over the commissioning of network programmes.

That led to the *Glasgow Herald*'s man asking for an example. I quoted the 13-part serial *The Standard*, based on life on a newspaper. When only six or seven of the programmes had been made in Scotland, London let it be known that there would be no second series. That had demoralised our staff. Yet if it had been a London programme a second series was almost certain, even if the first had not been perfect. In Scotland, I said, we had to achieve a higher standard than London's Television Centre demanded for itself. That was true; but used in a different context my words gave Managing Directors (tv and radio) Milne and Singer the opportunity to damn me in my annual report.

Those reports are a standard event in the BBC, usually made about once a year and written by someone either one or two levels above the individual. In my case, as Controller Scotland, my report was written by the two Managing Directors and presented to the Director General, who then discussed the report with me. Milne and Singer said that I had proved unfit to hold the post of Controller. In my view it was a harsh and damaging report and wholly unjust. But there had been distrust of a 'newspaper man' coming to a high post in the BBC, as I had done. And although Milne claimed a Scottish background, he seemed to have little sympathy for Scottish public attitudes of that time. I suspected that perhaps he, like many an expatriate, viewed Scotland only through the romantic mist of western islands, distant glens and the music of the pipes. I have quoted elsewhere (*Highlands and Islands: A Generation of Progress*, AUP 1989) the words of Ian MacArthur, sometime MP for East Perthshire: 'It is often quite easy, when considering the Highlands, to slip into a mood of romantic sentimentality. Like the reaction of the piper in Neil Munro's story, the heart leaps back over the years and yonder lies Glencoe. Romance and sentiment are very agreeable, but these emotions, which often cloud debate outside this House, distort judgment by obscuring reality with a tartan cloud ...'

The report embarrassed the DG, Ian Trethowan, when I had to appear before him in the late autumn. He said that I had perhaps pressed too hard in seeking more freedom for BBC Scotland and had been too ready to speak critically in public—as over the cancellation of the *Standard* series. As I had expected, Trethowan was both friendly to me and worried about what Milne and Singer had said. But he was standing back from my conflict with them. I believed that there was no justification for what they had said; but I was left with a feeling that neither BBC Scotland nor I were likely to receive the support from London that we needed. 'Autonomy' was far away, in spite of the Government's plans.

By this time it was clear to me that I ought to have insisted on a Directorate post from the start. That would have been closer to my *Guardian* position. But in my early talks with Sir Michael Swann that had seemed impossible, because of the opposition that would come from DG Curran. And since I had looked forward to the new job and wanted to return to Scotland, I did not force the point: in restrospect, possibly a mistake.

That autumn there were other factors diminishing the likelihood of great changes in Scottish affairs—factors in which BBC Scotland had no direct hand, but which exerted an important influence over subsequent events. First, there had been the fiasco of Scotland's swift defeat in the World Cup in Argentina, from which the Scottish team returned home humiliated. There had been wild expectations, as if the nation's self-esteem depended on its football (as noted in chapter 8), and there seemed to be a marked loss of national confidence. Less dramatic but more important, there was the closing of more shipyards, with a loss of jobs that extended far beyond shipbuilding as such. Then there was the seemingly perverse action of the Scottish National Party in voting with the Conservatives and against the Lib-Lab alliance of that period. The SNP did it in hope of winning more than half the Scottish seats at the coming elections, but in the event their tactics had the opposite effect. At the same time there was Lord Home's advice—a change of stance on his part—to 'Vote No' when the Referendum came. One other factor could be seen which affected the numbers voting against the Assembly: that was the unwillingness of people in the Highlands, the Islands, the Borders and to some extent Lothian to be ruled (as seemed likely) by the representatives of dominant Strathclyde.

By November, for better or worse, I had begun to doubt privately whether the Assembly would come at all. If it did not, then building the fine new BBC Broadcasting House for Edinburgh would almost certainly be cancelled. Radio Scotland was due to go on air at the end of the month, but that of itself was not enough to justify the Calton Hill building. Its construction had been delayed anyway, quite reasonably, to fit in with BBC financial planning.

That apart, our Broadcasting Council remained cheerful until they heard the new Radio Scotland at the end of the month. At its November meeting, early that month, the Council had gone so far as to commend a new television comedy series, *Scotch and Wry*, with the versatile Rikki Fulton in various roles. It introduced a fresh style in humour, new at least in Scotland, and we had expected some objections, since amongst other things it took a friendly swipe at religion. Not at all: the Rev. James Weatherhead, a relatively new member of the Council, thought very well of it. He remembered the trouble he himself had got into for saying that Noah was the first Do-It-Yourself boatbuilder—and he, like others, had much enjoyed the Rev I M Jolly's version of STV's 'Late Call'. (STV changed its style a little later.)

The December meeting was less cheerful, as noted in chapter 9. The BCS members did not like the new Radio Scotland. Although they had approved of the outline 18 months earlier—with our eyes on Radio Clyde's success and with our new station planned to be a mix of Radio 2 and Radio 4—they liked only the Radio 4 aspects. Ian Trethowan, arriving late to join the meeting, reassured them with his comments. That was much to my relief—and John Pickles's—but I had other reasons for being depressed that day. It was my own fault, and I knew that the DG was angry.

It happened because, a week or so earlier, I had sent a short note to each of the Broadcasting Council members with points that they might want to take up with the Director General. It was never my wish to embarrass Trethowan; it was only because the points were ones that I thought ought to be raised—

> Were we getting a fair deal on tv network drama? We knew that money was tight, not least because of the Government's restrictions, but we were getting even fewer network commissions than three years earlier.
>
> With the White Paper's commitment to let 'local' broadcasting remain with the BBC as well as ILR companies, when could we look for further part-time stations in the Borders and Dumfries? And was that to apply to Dundee? (The English local stations, with wider areas, were in continual competition with the ILR people.)
>
> While welcoming all the preparations for the Scottish Assembly, would our political staff be adequate for the task?

If my memory is correct, there were three further questions. They were all matters of importance to BBC Scotland. They were not intended to be traps for the DG, but it was a bad mistake on my part not to have sent a copy to him in advance. It would, indeed, have been more effective to have done so.

Two days before the meeting, David Barlow telephoned from London. He was now Chief Assistant, Regions, and as such he was to travel with the DG to Newcastle and on to Edinburgh. David wanted me to know that someone then working in Scotland had let the DG know about the list of questions, and Trethowan was angry. 'Get a copy to Newcastle as fast as you can', David said. So I got one off at once.

As a result, after his late arrival in Edinburgh and his brief comments on Radio Scotland as he had heard it on the the car radio coming north, the DG embarked on a series of comments. He included in his list most of my questions, but he stopped after each topic to invite comments from the BCS members. It was well done and lasted for almost ninety minutes.

He began with the forthcoming Referendum, mentioning a recent House of Commons debate in which the MP leading for the Scottish Nationalists had spoken well of me (to my embarrassment) but had gone on to say that when the time came his party would restructure *all* broadcasting in Scotland. For the record, the DG said, he wished to make clear that the BBC would take no part in any such restructuring. He then went on to what, in his view, were the two most important issues that day—the policy on staff payments and the retention of the licence fee as the BBC's main source of money. These were matters that were not on my list, and, quite properly, he spent some time on them.

Within that context, however, Trethowan mentioned the case of our planned Radio nan Eilean, to be run in Gaelic. He said that the offer from Comhairle nan Eilean (the Western Isles Council) to help finance the station was something that the BBC could accept. That applied not only to northern Scotland, and any such offers from the Borders or Dumfries would be similarly welcomed. So would offers in Wales. That answered one of my questions in part, and the matter of the part-time 'local' stations was covered immediately afterwards, to the satisfaction of the BCS members. So the meeting continued, though mainly on UK rather than Scottish affairs.

Later in the day Trethowan saw me by myself. He was very disappointed at what I had done, though the meeting had gone quite well. He wanted to say no more at present, except that I must come to see him in London the following week. At the weekend David Barlow telephoned to say that the DG had decided that I must go, but that he was truly upset about it. David asked if we might discuss the matter before I saw Trethowan and we agreed to have lunch in London two days later, before the DG saw me.

The swift despatch was a surprise, and a satisfaction for Milne and Singer. I had won the *Lilybank* battle a year earlier, to Milne's irritation, but had lost the bigger conflict now. I had believed that BBC Scotland should be more active in reporting social and political affairs and in promoting debate. We had achieved that quite quickly, and we were ready for whatever might come with the Assembly. What I had done in speaking out for Scotland's interests had undoubtedly annoyed the hierarchy in London, but it was hardly a heinous crime. I had handled the matter of the DG's visit to the Broadcasting Council tactlessly, though few would have regarded it as a matter for resignation. But I had always been regarded as a journalist cuckoo in the broadcasting nest and much resented for this reason. And by now I was tired of the battling, bickering and back-stabbing that seemed to be endemic within the upper echelons of the BBC, and weary of the endless journeys to and from London, often for useless meetings.

During my years at *The Guardian* I had fought a long battle to preserve that newspaper's identity and to prevent its merger with *The Times*, as reported in my book *Guardian Years* (Chatto and Windus, 1981). That had seemed to me a worthy fight. Now I simply felt despair at dealing with constant petty-mindedness. Leaving the job would almost come as a relief.

Meanwhile I had to do some thinking. I could have been difficult, demanding financial compensation. (My contract still had three years to go, and my pension was to be a fraction of what it would have been if I had stayed with *The Guardian*.) But I did not want a public row. Instead I wanted to do something interesting and useful. The post of Station Manager at Inverness was vacant. Why not go there, and return to real journalism?

When David Barlow heard of this at lunch in London he was sure that the DG would jump at the suggestion. He cut short his lunch and went to brief Trethowan. The DG accepted it at once. He was clearly upset: we had almost always got on well. But it was obvious that he had taken account of what Milne and Singer had said two months earlier. It was quite a short meeting that day (13 December 1978), but because I was due to leave for Egypt next day it was agreed that there would be no announcement until after I returned the following week. A small irony: at a much later date both Milne and Singer were removed from their posts—Singer by Milne (then the DG) and Milne by the Governors.

Sorry as I was at being removed from my job, Inverness had attractions. It was a part of Scotland that I loved, and it would mean occasional visits to the west coast and the outer isles. It would free me from all the worries as Controller, and it meant that I could go back to the kind of work as a journalist that I had done on the *Glasgow Herald* 35 years before. Ian Trethowan also decided that I should remain a member of a committee in London that was trying to forecast what the BBC would be doing ten years ahead—and that meant a flight to London once a month, allowing me to visit my young daughters, who were still at school.

The visit to Egypt was for the recce for the eighth of *Mountain Days*. The crew was to be, as far as possible, the same as on *Three Men on the Goat* and the producer, David Hanley, and director Mike Radford had already gone ahead of me. They were to meet me at Luxor, well up the Nile, and we were then to go by road to Hurghada, on the Red Sea. They had had a good look at Luxor before I arrived, in case we needed any shots there, but the main target was Hadrian's Mountain. As already noted, it was known as Hadrian's Mountain because he had been in command there before coming to Britain. The hard rock below the mountains, composed of white and red crystals, was then being dug out and sent to Rome for the building of the Colosseum.

My awareness of those mountains was accidental. Twelve years earlier I had been to Egypt to interview Nasser on the tenth anniversary of the Suez war. He insisted that before leaving I must go to see the Aswan Dam, then under construction. When I was flying back to Cairo the plane was diverted up the Red Sea because of a very unusual storm. As it passed over those amazing mountains close to Hurghada I decided that some day I must try to go there. Much later, when Egypt was about to come to terms with Israel, in 1978, I had spoken to the Egyptian Ambassador in London, whom I had known in the past. He was enthusiastic, because his country hoped to develop tourist business on the Red Sea shores as soon as the Egypt-Israel peace terms were settled. He said that their army would provide a four-wheel vehicle so that we could get through the sands to Hadrian's base. The peace terms had been expected in November, but finally came early in the following year.

Meanwhile Mike Radford, David Hanley and I set off by the old British road, built in 1940, running from north of Luxor to Safaga, a large port south of Hurghada. Before leaving home I had obtained pills to prevent malaria, and I understood that the pills should be taken from the time of arrival in Egypt. Hanley and Radford had been advised to start taking their pills before leaving Scotland. Anyway, we covered the 150 or so miles in a hired car with driver, but we had lunch at a squalid stopping place—the only one on the route—where I was badly bitten. We then went on to the coast, passing the south-west side of Hadrian's Mountain (7175 feet, apparently), wonderful to see in morning and evening light. Having passed through three army check-points on the way, we were stopped by the police at Hurghada and required to stay in a sort of prison—actually a house where we could be indoors, out of the the burning sun or in a small garden, until the Military Commander arrived. Luckily for us, he spoke English and he was mystified that no advance warning of our coming had been sent from Cairo. He decided to put us into the only hotel, half-built, by the shore not far away—with a warning that the beach was mined. Technically, the Egyptians were still at war.

From the hotel, towards sunset and again in the morning, the view was magnificent—a collection of small islands out to sea, our mountains to the west, and to the north-east, 85 miles away, there stood the Monastery of St Catherine and above it the 7497 feet summit of Sinai. At midday we could see only a short way because of the heat. In the morning the Commander came to see us. The relevant people in Cairo knew all about us and had said that we should be given all possible help, but the army's four-wheel vehicles could not be made available because they must stay at battle stations. If we could wait until the peace had been signed, everything possible would be done to help ... All we could do was to try to walk, to see what the ground was like. With the gruelling heat and no easy way of getting across the sand, we soon gave up. We never reached Hadrian's temple, but morning and evening we could watch those huge hills, with their three spires double the size of Sgurr nan Gillean.

On the plane going back home I began to feel unreal. It was the beginning of malaria, though I did not know it at the time. The next few days were a daze and I have little recollection of them. A day or two after I got back to Glasgow my resignation was announced. I delivered a short farewell talk to those of the Glasgow staff who chose to come—a great many, I am told. My opening words were 'Yes, you are going to have a new Controller, and I wish him the very best of luck.'

After that, malaria took over until well into January, when I moved to Inverness. Meanwhile I received an unexpected number of letters, all kind and regretful.

Addendum

It had its benefits: I enjoyed Radio Highland. I had no real worries. The management and administration were almost all done by Tom Prag, the number two, who was also a first class broadcaster (and more recently Managing Director of Moray Firth Radio). The Gaels, who produced half the output from Radio Highland, were a lively and amusing lot. So, for that matter, were the non-Gaelic staff—nearly all young and vigorous. They were a fine group to work with.

There was another benefit. In Inverness, in late spring, I met my second wife, Sheila Cameron, recently widowed. We shared much the same interests and Sheila's three children were almost the same ages as my four, but it was perhaps the loneliness of personal grief that first drew us together. Miranda, my first wife, had decided just before I moved to Glasgow that she did not want to come—a severe shock and sadness to me at the time. She had recently qualified as a social worker, and she wanted to stay in her job in South London. Our two sons were at or approaching university level, and the two girls were still at school in London. Happily, over the years I was able to stay at Miranda's house, with the children, more or less as often as I wished.

Sheila and I were married in the autumn. She joined me in some new activities after I left Radio Highland in the spring of 1980. We made a number of TV programmes for the new Channel 4. She also helped me with much of my work (half-time) as a research professor at Stirling University; and she helped me in writing a number of books, as well as writing her own: a biography of the Duchess of Atholl, Scotland's first woman MP. Without her, this book would never have been written. Once or twice a year as many as possible of Sheila's children, my children, and our grandchildren, with Miranda and her second husband John Beavis, gather somewhere in Scotland or Northern England. That we all enjoy.

> Alastair Hetherington
> High Corrie
> Isle of Arran

Appendix 1

Costs of departments, BBC Scotland

An indication of costs for our departments, taken from the network BBC 1 and BBC 2 'accepted' programmes on 6 April 1978 for the year April '78 to March '79.

Drama	£283K network and £21K local.
News	£170K approx. (£53K for staff and overheads; plus £97K for programme costs.)
Current Affairs, Documentaries and Conference (political) cover	£184K of which current affairs £57K local and £35K network; documentaries and features £44K network and £40K local; conferences £7.5K local.
Light Entertainment	£66K local and £52K network.
Religion	£63K local and £5K network.
Music and Arts	£85K local and £21K network.
Sports and Events	£46K local and £10K network (estimated).
Agriculture	£37K (estimated).
Gaelic	£23K (estimated).

Those were not far from the ultimate costs.

Appendix 2

All figures in millions

	Year	Scotland	Wales	N. Ireland	UK totals
Income					
To BBC from licence fees, after Home Office charges	74–75	13.0	6.9	2.4	147.3
	75–76	18.9	9.9	3.0	214.4
	76–77	20.7	10.8	3.2	227.0
	77–78	23.9	12.5	3.8	261.8
Operating Costs					
After deducting, for regions, network pgms, made by them, TV	75–75	2.9	3.2	1.3	—
	75–76	2.9	3.8	1.8	—
	76–77	Not available	Not available		
Share of network pgms and other costs, TV, as charged from London	74–75	8.9	4.9	2.0	97.9
	75–76	10.8	5.6	1.9	118.6
	76–77	Not available	Not available		
TV total	74–75	11.7	8.1	3.3	108.9
	75–76	13.7	9.4	3.7	131.8
	76–77	Not available	Not available		

Radio, after deduction of network pgms made in regions	74–75	1.4	1.2	0.7	—
	75–76	1.8	1.5	1.0	—
	76–77	Not available			
Share of network pgms charges and other costs, radio	74–75	3.0	1.6	0.7	33.3
	75–76	3.7	2.0	0.7	42.2
	76–77	Not available			
Capital expenditure	74–75	1.3	0.7	0.2	12.3
	75–76	1.6	0.8	0.3	17.8
	76–77	Not available			
Surplus/deficit	74–75	−4.4	−4.7	−2.6	−17.5
	75–76	−1.9	−3.9	−2.6	−12.4
	76–77	−4.2	−5.6	−3.5	−3.5
	77–78	−5.6	−5.7	−4.0	n.a.

Note, however, that the basis on which Scotland, Wales and N. Ireland were charged for receiving network programmes, tv and radio, was never revealed.

Note also that, at that time, 625UH coloured tv had not yet reached substantial parts of Scotland; and that the BBC so far had weathered the Government's restrictions on the licence fee because it had a reserve of some £80 millions.